"ALWAYS CONSIDER THE DESIGN OF A THING IN ITS NEXT LARGER CONTEXT – A CHAIR IN A ROOM, A ROOM IN A HOUSE, A HOUSE IN AN ENVIRONMENT, AN ENVIRONMENT IN A CITY PLAN."

THE HOME
BUYER'S GUIDE

what to **look** & **ask** for
when buying a new home

CONTENTS

PREFACE

Life is full of momentous milestones –
your first steps as a toddler; your first
day at school; your first kiss; your first pint.
Perhaps one milestone that unites us all,
regardless of ethnicity, gender or age, is the
first time we buy a home.

How many of our memories are wrapped
up in our homes? After our flesh and blood,
it is the one thing in which we invest most
of our emotional capital, as well as most of
our financial resources. Yet some people put
more care into choosing and planning
where they want to go on holiday than
they do into deciding which home they are
going to buy.

When it comes to choosing your home, you
have got to be careful. Once you've moved
in, you can't turn around and ask for your
money back if you discover there is
something that you don't like. And if you –
like many others – are choosing to buy a
home off-plan, you will need to be extra
vigilant, and make sure you get what you
want from your builder.

We all have to start demanding more,
raising expectations and coercing builders
into building homes that suit our needs.
What we want are well-designed, carefully
planned and expertly delivered homes
with an after care service better than the
best car dealers.

If I was buying a newly built home, this is what I would want to be able to do:

→ step out of my front door into a wonderfully landscaped streetscape and say hello to my neighbours

→ have a kick about with my kids or mates in a nearby communal area

→ have a well-designed home that is much, much more than an identikit rabbit hutch

→ have a choice of interior layouts, a choice of kitchens, sensible radiator positioning and an efficient after sales service.

On the high street, at the supermarket or in the car showroom, we have come to expect great design, product perfection and wonderful service. We can buy amazing, innovative products to use inside and outside our homes. When it comes to buying a home, however, these expectations aren't always met.

This book will help you to identify quality homes, and help you to demand more. Don't feel afraid to make more work for house builders, estate agents or marketing teams. Ultimately, it is your emotional and financial capital that will be invested in the home.

Wayne Hemingway

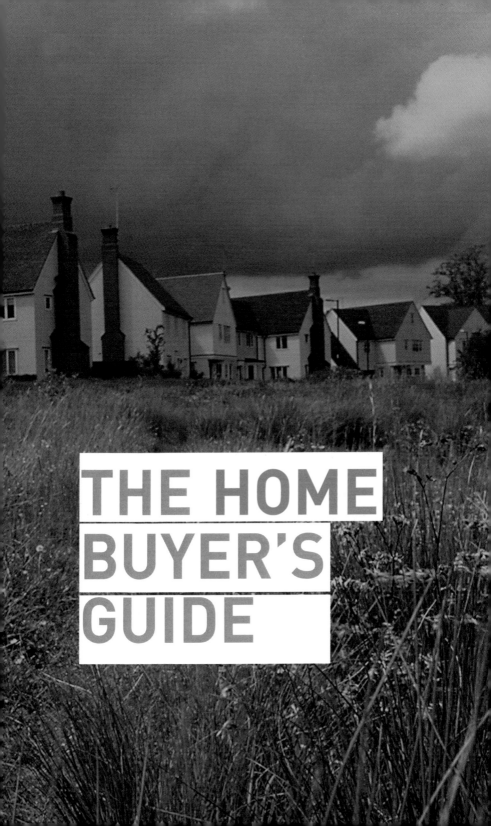

THE HOME BUYER'S GUIDE

INTRODUCTION

This guide is about everything that makes a well-designed home. That doesn't just mean how to use space, how best to light a room or the importance of built-in storage. It is also about the space outside of the home, about how to identify a well-designed neighbourhood or how public and private spaces interact. Its intention is to help you ensure that the home you are buying is of the standard that you deserve.

There are many factors that will impact both on the price and, more importantly, the cost of your home. You might wonder what the difference is. Well, the price is what you pay on exchange of contracts. The cost of your home is how much money you'll spend on it during the time you live there. A well-designed home is going to cost you a lot less than a badly designed one.

A good neighbourhood, for example, will cost you a lot less, in terms of travel, if you can walk to work or to your local shops. A home with the latest insulation techniques will significantly reduce your heat consumption. Housing developments where private and public spaces have been thoughtfully planned together will create a

better sense of community and, as a result, reduce the likelihood of crime, making them safer places in which to live.

This guide will help you to identify homes that have been well-designed, as well as highlighting some examples of poor practice. It starts by discussing the key elements that comprise a neighbourhood, and moves on to look at the internal elements within a well-designed home. Finally, it sets out some key issues relating to the spaces around your new home, including gardens, car parking and bin storage.

You might want to sit down and read this guide all in one go. More likely, you will probably just dip in, as and when you've got the time. Within each section there are a series of questions that you should ask of the property you may be considering buying, as well as things that you should be on the look-out for. There are some really outstanding examples of new homes out there, some of which are highlighted here. With the help of this guide, you will be better able to find a new home that suits your needs and expectations.

"OUR HOUSES ARE SUCH UNWIELDY PROPERTY THAT WE ARE OFTEN IMPRISONED RATHER THAN HOUSED IN THEM."

Sustainability – what is that all about?

Well, it doesn't mean that you have to put solar panels and wind turbines all over your home. What *sustainability* refers to is the need to build homes which meet our immediate needs, whilst not depriving future generations of enjoying similar standards of living. Sustainable homes should be well-designed, safe, accessible, adaptable and cost-effectively built. A sustainable development will contribute to a higher quality of life, by making effective use of natural resources, protecting the environment, promoting social cohesion and strengthening the economy.

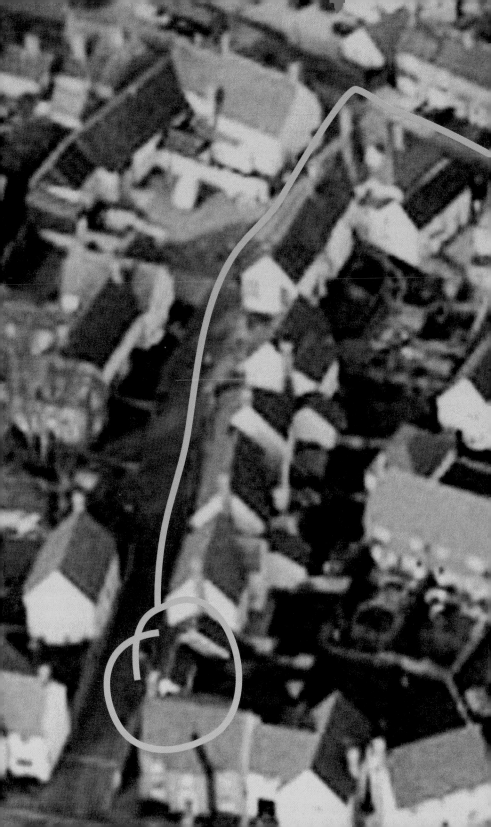

LOCATION

THE LOCATION OF YOUR HOME ISN'T JUST ITS
POSITION ON A MAP. IT'S MUCH MORE THAN THAT.
A WELL-DESIGNED NEIGHBOURHOOD WILL HAVE A
SENSE OF CHARACTER THAT IS MORE THAN ESTATE
AGENT'S SPIN, STREET LAYOUTS THAT WORK FOR
PEOPLE (AND THEIR CARS) AND A RANGE OF
HOUSING TYPES TO SUIT ALL OUR NEEDS.

THINK OUTSIDE THE BOX

When an estate agent tells you about the latest addition to their portfolio, they will no doubt talk about a home with 'character' that is in a 'pleasant neighbourhood'. More than likely, you'll nod your head and eagerly agree to visit the property, because these factors are, after all, just what you're looking for.

Or are they? If you asked the estate agent for their definition of a 'characterful' home would it bear any resemblance to your own requirements? If you want to know about their views on 'pleasant neighbourhoods', it is more than likely they will trot out the old adage about the importance of 'location, location, location'.

But it is not as simple as that. A neighbourhood should improve your quality of life, the value of your property, your sense of privacy and security, and help to create a community with your neighbours. Or, to put it another way, it is all about 'location, location, design'.

Do you ever go on holiday to a Tuscan hill village or a French market town and find yourself asking why your neighbourhood can't feel as they do?

Location can have as much impact on the resale value of your home as the property itself.

It is interesting to compare aerial views. The photo on the left is of Edinburgh, showing the character of the city defined by a variety of terraces and crescents. Homes sit comfortably next to business and retail outlets, and there is plenty of green space. By contrast the image on the right is marked by isolated parcels of housing, superstores and business parks, surrounded by asphalt and car parking. It's not the kind of place you might visit for a weekend, let alone choose to live.

It can be difficult to pinpoint what it is about some places that makes them desirable and attractive. Often such places have many things in common. They have a sense of identity and character which is particular to place. Think about Cambridge where character is achieved by its mixture and variety of architecture, or Bath and Edinburgh where the built environment has a sense of order and homogeneity, while at the same time being varied, with terraces, crescents, parks and squares.

Note: words in italic throughout this guide refer to a useful glossary of terms on page 104.

Another factor that makes a well-designed neighbourhood is ease of navigation, with streets that connect instead of confuse and local landmarks, such as a church or monument, which aid orientation. Finally, the well-designed neighbourhood will include properties that have been sited to maximise security and safety, and minimise energy use.

Ultimately, you should be able to describe where you live as a place in its own right, rather than an apparently random collection of unconnected, and rather dull boxes.

This development has character because it is compact, with a variety of housing types connected by meandering streets and pathways.

Modern housing needn't mean dull noddy boxes. It can have the character and variety of places that have grown over time.

NEIGHBOURHOOD

Density

Units per hectare

All the positive examples of neighbourhoods in this guide contain over 40 homes per *hectare*. You will see that higher densities needn't compromise the quality of space or the provision of a variety of homes, including detached family houses.

What are the benefits of higher density?

- reasonable proximity to your neighbours helps build a sense of community
- it improves the viability of, and access to, community services
- it supports public transport and reduces car travel
- it increases *energy efficiency*
- it reduces overall demand for development land.

Market towns

These tend to be built to densities of 50-70 units per *hectare*. The top ten most successful and popular market towns today, according to the Campaign to Protect Rural England are:

- Tavistock, Devon
- Easingwold, North Yorkshire
- Frome, Somerset
- Saffron Walden, Essex
- Maldon, Essex
- Market Bosworth, Leicestershire
- Skipton, North Yorkshire
- Wimborne, Dorset
- Longridge, Lancashire
- Ludlow, Shropshire

In order for a post office and pub to survive financially they require a surrounding population of about 7,000 people. And with only 2.33 people inside today's average home, that works out at almost 4,300 properties. If there were 40 homes on each *hectare*, you'd have no problem walking to the post office. But at 20 properties to a *hectare*, you're looking at the possibility of a 1.5 km journey each way.

A successful neighbourhood of reasonable density will not only be able to support a post office and pub, but also a local school, public transport links, a take-away and even a bingo hall. So, although you might not have thought of asking about the *density per hectare* of your dream location, it is worth keeping such a question in mind. Remember, the closer you are to your neighbour, the closer you are likely to be to a bus stop, sports facilities and shops.

To give you an idea of what this means Brookside Close is approximately 20 homes per *hectare*, whilst Albert Square is around 75. Perhaps this is why the latter has the Queen Vic and a vibrant community scene, and why the former was unsustainable – and is no longer on air.

Coin Street, London

Coin Street is a hugely successful development. The old OXO building has been converted to house artists' workshops with affordable housing above them, along with a rooftop restaurant. Next to it is a new terrace of family homes with a public landscaped park. The neighbouring Iroko building is made up of apartments and maisonettes set around a shared landscaped garden.

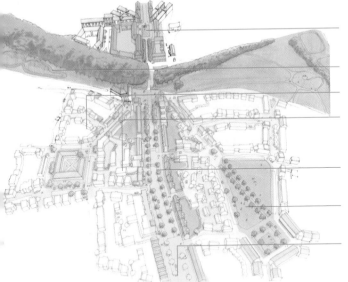

new village centre with crêche and doctor's surgery

ecology park

squares and gardens

mixture of mews houses, courtyard houses, terraced and detached homes

formal boulevard with town houses and apartments

pocket park and children's play area

bus links to town and footpath to local schools

New Hall, Harlow

The Abode housing is part of a large new development at New Hall that has been designed to include a new neighbourhood centre with a doctor's surgery and nursery which will serve the new residents, as well as those living in the surrounding area. The development also incorporates an ecology park and children's play areas. The local school is within walking distance of homes in the area and the development has bus connections to Harlow town centre. New Hall will have a mixture of detached family homes, mews housing, apartments and *live/work units* to encourage local people to set up businesses from their homes.

Use

If you have a pub, a local shop, a take-away and, perhaps a post office, then you are going to be living in a vibrant area. However, this could mean potential tensions between the local businesses and the neighbourhood's inhabitants. There's nothing more annoying than being awakened by an early morning delivery on your day off. Goods yards and delivery areas need to be incorporated into the design of a neighbourhood, so as to avoid noise, and disruption. So, if there are businesses in the area where you're looking to buy, make sure that you think about how their operations might affect your lifestyle now, and in the future, and how well designed the neighbourhood is in order to minimise disturbance.

Mix it

Now you know that the area can accommodate your current needs, what about your needs in five years time? What about the changing needs of your family? What if your fortunes take a turn for the better – or worse? A sustainable neighbourhood will contain housing that can accommodate individuals and families on a range of incomes, and with a range of needs. It should include a wide variety of property sizes so that if you have children you can stay in the neighbourhood and when they leave home you should be able to trade down, using the spare cash you will earn for a winter cruise or the like. It will incorporate privately owned property, *intermediate ownership* (where you part own and part rent a property) and rental properties. It will also include housing of different styles. Such a mix – known as mixed *tenure* – helps to support viable neighbourhood facilities with something for everyone.

WHAT TO ASK	WHAT TO LOOK FOR
→ What public transport links are there.	→ A place of character with a sense of identity.
→ Where are the local schools – and how good are they.	→ Accessible public parks and green spaces.
→ Does the local authority have any future development plans for the area.	→ Well maintained public facilities.
→ If so, will they bring benefits to the neighbourhood – or disruptions to it.	→ A mixture of local amenities, including a doctor's surgery and local shop – and, perhaps, a post office.

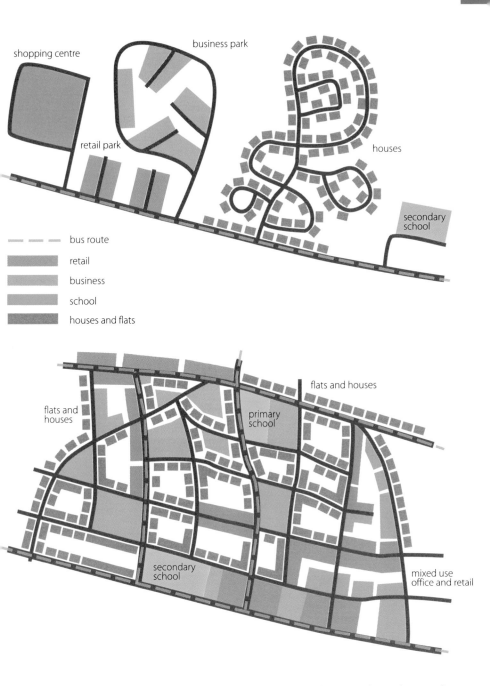

shopping centre

business park

retail park

houses

secondary school

bus route
retail
business
school
houses and flats

flats and houses

flats and houses

primary school

secondary school

mixed use office and retail

Compare the illustrations of neighbourhood layouts above. The top illustration shows the sort of development we saw happening in the 1980s – business parks separated from supermarkets separated from isolated housing estates.

The lower illustration shows a layout that tends to result in a more successful neighbourhood. Housing, businesses, schools and retail outlets are more closely related, with better routes and networks connecting them, resulting in less congestion and better access.

This illustration, of a local neighbourhood, shows amenities which are within a five minute and a ten minute walk of the home at the centre.

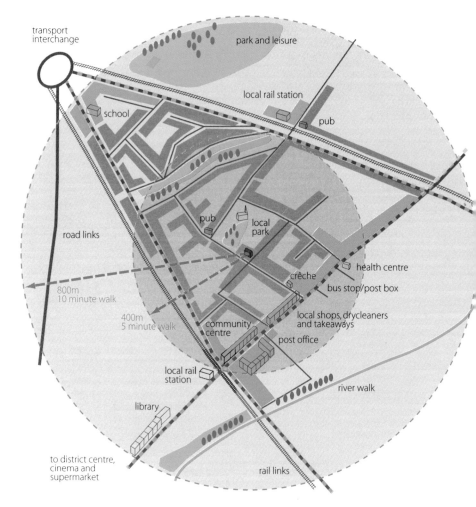

transport interchange

park and leisure

local rail station

school

pub

road links

pub

local park

health centre

crèche

bus stop/post box

800m
10 minute walk

400m
5 minute walk

community centre

local shops, drycleaners and takeaways

post office

local rail station

river walk

library

to district centre, cinema and supermarket

rail links

bus route

retail and business

houses and apartments

Five minute walk

More people equals more shops, more chance of a doctor's surgery or hairdresser's staying in business for longer than six months.

We all know that a bicycle shed is where you park your bike. A 'pedshed', however, is not a place to park your feet. Instead, it describes the distance that you would be prepared to walk in order to reach local amenities. A pedshed is everything within 400 metres of your home. So when you're looking at properties, you should consider a five minute walk in any direction from the property, keeping an eye out for transport links, play areas, shops, post boxes and recycling facilities. Along main roads and at crossroads there tends to be a higher concentration of activity particularly shops, and these should be within a 10 minute or 800 metre walk from your home.

The thought of owning your first home and getting onto the first rung of the property ladder can result in you rushing your home buying decision. It is important, though, to think outside the box and consider these neighbourhood elements as they will have a big impact on your quality of life.

What are the benefits of living in a *mixed use* area?

- more convenient access to facilities
- rush hour congestion is minimised
- greater opportunity for social interaction
- a variety of architecture
- a greater feeling of safety, with more 'eyes on the street'
- greater *energy efficiency* and more efficient use of space and buildings
- vitality of street life
- increased viability of facilities and support for small businesses, such as a corner shop.

STREET

Get connected

The average commuting time is now 40 per cent higher than it was 20 years ago. And car traffic is predicted to increase by a further 35 per cent by 2025. The rise in car use has presented designers and architects with one of their biggest challenges.

Some early housing developments by visionary architects sought to separate cars and pedestrians through the use of elevated walkways above roads. Others, who designed developments according to *Radburn principles*, positioned roads and garages together on one side of houses and footpaths on the other. While these approaches were perfectly rational, the separation of cars and pedestrians often created confusion about private and public space. At times this has resulted in footpaths becoming magnets for crime and car parks attracting vandalism.

In some cases – for example, at the Brunswick Centre in London – the use of elevated walkways and underground service roads works. These public areas are well managed and maintained by the estate. The benefit of this approach can be seen in the positive transformation of problem estates following the introduction of concierges and secure access.

A footpath might provide a useful shortcut, but if it's not overlooked by surrounding buildings or well lit, it can be an unappealing route to have to take, particularly after dark.

The Brunswick Centre, London and Queen Elizabeth Park, Guildford, both illustrate successful examples of *Radburn principles* with separated pedestrian and vehicle access.

The best model for creating safe and vibrant public areas is through a network of linked streets. Successfully connected streets not only help journeys made by car, they also make it easier to get from A to B on foot. By contrast, dead-end street networks, such as cul-de-sacs, limit your choice of travel, frustrating your journey. Ultimately, successful housing developments have streets and footpaths that are connected to existing routes and neighbourhoods, thereby creating a district that is *permeable* and easily negotiable by foot or car.

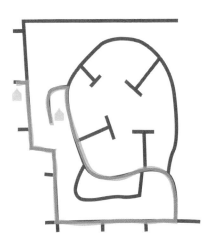

This street layout shows a typical cul-de-sac with dead-end streets. The cul-de-sac fails to integrate with its surroundings. A journey from A to B is a long convoluted one. It is not easy to walk to neighbourhood facilities, making car journeys much more likely.

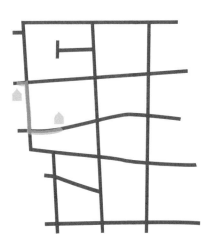

This street layout shows a linked network of streets, a more pedestrian friendly approach that connects new streets to existing ones. Here the journey from A to B is short, obvious and direct, encouraging people to walk to local shops and neighbourhood facilities.

When we walk out of our homes most of us want to be able to mix with our neighbours or look across a pleasant street. Too often, the design of housing has been determined by the demands of the road system, to the neglect of the creation of a sense of place.

If you happen to bump into someone while walking down the street, it will usually result in an apology or perhaps a polite conversation. A similar incident between two cars, however, is more likely to lead to anxiety, rage or hospitalisation. And an accident involving cars and people is, of course, going to be worse – indeed, half of all road accidents involving children under the age of five happen within 100 metres of their home. So, a well-designed development should achieve a balance between the rights of the pedestrian and the car driver, with streets that are established as public spaces, and not solely as the domain of the car.

A people friendly street will make walking and cycling safe, pleasant and convenient, creating a sense of harmony between pedestrians and drivers. By careful consideration of street landscaping, well-designed developments can ensure that car speeds are kept to a minimum, thereby providing safe, vibrant environments for children to play and neighbours to meet and chat.

Home Zone

Home Zone describes a shared space between and around properties that are designed to balance the needs of the pedestrian and community with the demands made by the car. Good landscaping, chicanes, trees and seating areas help to limit car speeds and create a place for pedestrians to enjoy themselves.

A traditional street layout where the houses frame the street while also helping to define it.

Is your street child friendly?

ompare these two developments. The one on the left has a broad expanse of tarmac that encourages rivers to speed and creates an unattractive landscape that seems to have been designed only with the ar in mind. The development on the right has been designed to slow down car traffic, creating a street at is both attractive and a place where people can meet and children play safely.

Pocket parks

Any spare space in a city or between buildings has the potential to be a park, even if it is just a place to kick a ball, read a newspaper or hang out with friends. Ideally, *'pocket parks'* should be at strategic locations – at the corner of a street, in a square, or by a canal or river. If well designed they provide shelter, seating and soften otherwise hard environments.

WHAT TO ASK

→ Ask neighbours if there are any particular noise issues that might affect your privacy, whether heavy road traffic at certain times of day, busy railways nearby, or flight paths overhead.

WHAT TO LOOK FOR

→ A street layout that is well connected.

→ A street layout that incorporates a balance between the needs of the pedestrian and the car driver.

→ Streets that are overlooked by housing – these will be safer.

→ Streets with narrow sections or tight turns – to help reduce car speeds.

→ Good street lighting.

→ Visit the area at different times of day to see if changing traffic levels affect your enjoyment of the area.

The distance from your front door to the property on the opposite side of the street has a profound effect on the number of neighbours you are likely to get to know. In a compact terraced street you may not have your own forecourt for parking, but the benefits of being close to neighbours usually outweighs not being able to park directly in front of your home. In a well-designed neighbourhood, residents are able to supervise their children as they play outside, with other residents not being disturbed by the children's games.

A street feels right if properties are designed to create a sense of enclosure and continuity, that is to say that they follow 'the line of the street' and relate to each other. A property at the end of a row of terraced houses should overlook the street at its front, as well as at its side. A blank wall without windows is more likely to provide a blank canvas for graffiti and, obviously, won't let in any natural light. If footpaths and streets are overlooked by houses, they are more likely to make those people walking on them – as well as car drivers using them – feel safer. Street lighting also plays a part here. Where street lighting improvements have been made neighbourhoods have seen reductions in crime levels and the fear of crime.

Kill your speed
Accommodating pedestrians and enforcing reduced speed limits across the UK's residential areas would save around 13,000 children a year from death or injury, while creating 20km ph zones in all appropriate residential streets would prevent an estimated 50,000 casualties a year.

Holly Street, London
When the Holly Street Housing Estate, in London, was redeveloped from a single *tenure* housing estate to mixed *tenure* incorporating a community centre, shops and doctor's surgery, the safety of the area improved. The new neighbourhood has a more *permeable* network of streets and squares. Interviews with residents show that fear associated with the area dropped from 60 per cent to just 16 per cent. The proportion of people witnessing a violent incident fell from 44 per cent to 2 per cent and thefts outside the home dropped from 28 per cent to 1 per cent.

THE POSITION OF YOUR HOME

Orientation

When you choose your home, you need to remember that its orientation will have a bearing on the quality of light, the degree of privacy and security – and the *energy efficiency* of your property.

Not all properties can face south – often perceived to be the best orientation – but a well-designed home will optimise the benefits of the sun and be sheltered from the impact of the prevailing wind, further helping to reduce heat loss. South facing windows help to improve the *energy efficiency* of a home, because solar energy warms the walls and floors of a building. North facing windows, meanwhile, offer a more even quality of light, which is why artists often like their studios to face north.

While homes should be designed to take advantage of the sun, the design should also ensure that this exposure is not overwhelming. Overhanging eaves, balconies, shades or a trellis can provide necessary shade in the summer when the sun is high, but should not obstruct the sun in the winter when the sun is low. Another thing to remember when you are visiting your potential new home is that a property orientated to make the most of the sun will produce comparative energy savings of about 10 per cent.

At the New Hall development in Harlow, the architects insisted that all the homes should benefit from direct sun. The Abode houses have big picture windows and built-in conservatories. Windows are shaded with external timber louvres or have balconies above them.

Each of the houses in this terrace in Hockerton, Nottinghamshire, has a large triple glazed conservatory, bringing the dual benefits of passive solar gain and plenty of light into each home.

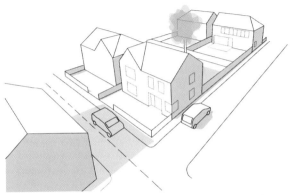

It is worth trying to anticipate how the changing angle of the sun and surrounding buildings will affect your home. Remember the angle of the sun is at its lowest in winter and will cast long shadows, while the summer sun is higher, so overshadowing will be reduced.

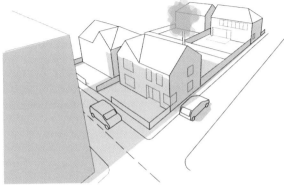

Here we see the impact of a shadow cast at midday in spring or autumn. In the top illustration the middle house is unaffected by the shadow cast by a house of similar size, positioned due south of it. In the bottom illustration, an apartment block with two extra storeys in the same position will deprive the middle house of direct sun for most of the year.

BedZed in Sutton has been designed to be as energy efficient as possible. Each property has living rooms facing south, while a conservatory captures solar energy heating the walls and floor of the building. Electricity and heating are provided by solar panels incorporated into the design of each home.

WHAT TO ASK	WHAT TO LOOK FOR	
→ Which way is south and which rooms receive direct light at what time of the day.	→ Are rooms orientated to take advantage of the sun.	→ Are there any features that prevent the overheating of rooms such as trees, external shades or balconies above.
	→ Does the morning sun shine into the bedroom or onto the breakfast table.	
		→ Are there other buildings or planting that shelter the house from the prevailing wind.
	→ Does the evening sun shine into the living room.	

Security and privacy

The positioning of your home will have a bearing on your sense of safety and privacy. A property with rooms overlooking a street may have less privacy, but it will provide greater security.

Most new housing developments have incorporated privacy issues into their design. Some might have 'Secured by Design' status, which signals that they have incorporated high walls at the back of the houses with low open views at the front.

Secured by Design

A study of 27 housing estates in West Yorkshire designed according to 'Secured by Design' principles, reported that crime rates had dropped between 54 per cent and 67 per cent. The number of burglaries was half that of other West Yorkshire estates and there were 42 per cent fewer vehicle crimes. The average cost of the extra design measures was £440 per new dwelling compared to average burglary losses of £1,670 per dwelling.

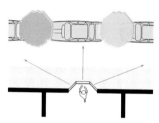

A window on the corner of a building overlooks the street on both sides and brings additional light into the home.

A bay window over-looking the street provides views in three directions.

A well-designed home will have its windows suitably located to take advantage of views of the surrounding landscape, street or rooftops.

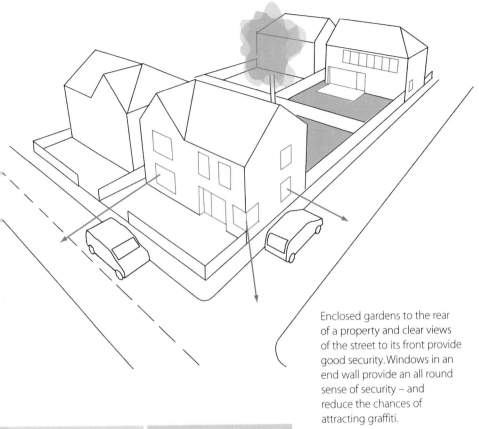

Enclosed gardens to the rear of a property and clear views of the street to its front provide good security. Windows in an end wall provide an all round sense of security – and reduce the chances of attracting graffiti.

WHAT TO ASK

→ Does the development have '*Secured by Design*' accreditation, or does it adopt these principles.

→ Does the property have any special security features.

→ What are the crime rates like in the area – you could visit www.upmystreet.com as a first point of call.

WHAT TO LOOK FOR

→ Windows in the property that overlook public areas, footpaths and streets.

→ Alleyways or shared spaces at the back of the property should be well lit and secure.

→ A home designed to benefit from the best available views.

→ Easy escape routes in the event of a fire.

HOME
DESIGN

ONCE YOU HAVE FOUND THE RIGHT LOCATION, YOU WILL NEED TO START LOOKING AT PROPERTY. BIG, SMALL, WIDE, THIN. WHICHEVER TICKLES YOUR FANCY, YOU WILL NEED TO BEAR IN MIND A NUMBER OF DESIGN ISSUES – FROM ENERGY EFFICIENCY TO THE USE OF SPACE, LIGHTING OPTIONS TO STORAGE SOLUTIONS.

THE PLEASURE PRINCIPLE

Think of some of the small pleasures that you can get from your home, like seeing sunlight slowly spread across your living room floor. Or being able to open your windows to let in the summer sun or close the shutters to block out the winter chill. Or having the space to display a cherished piece of furniture. A well-designed home will let you experience these pleasures – and, hopefully, many more.

Can you measure delight? When it comes to other aspects of design – such as flexibility, durability and *sustainability* – all you need to do is to ask for the statistics. After all, you would expect this information if you were buying a car – so why not when you are buying a property? Your seller should be able to tell you the floor area, *build specification*, energy rating and running costs, as well as whether there is any after sales service provided. What they won't be able to tell you is the happiness quotient that comes from a well-designed home.

Better by design

The University of Bristol carried out a survey of 600 households on a large suburban estate with little or no distinctive design quality. The researchers found that not only did these residents have more difficulty in selling their homes, they also experienced more *negative equity* than those living on more distinctly designed developments.

Everyone has opinions on what architectural styles they like, but good design can be judged objectively. A well-designed home is not just about its external appearance. It must be sustainable. It should be safe, efficient and affordable. The use of space, storage and light will all contribute to its overall design quality. In addition, it should be able to adapt or expand according to your changing circumstances.

If these elements are present, then the well-designed home you are looking to buy will not only be a wise financial investment, but will also add value to your quality of life.

If you are struggling to get onto the property ladder you might think that you can't afford good design as well as a roof over your head. In spite of what many developers say, however, good design doesn't need to cost more. A home orientated to catch the sun doesn't cost more to build than one facing north. The same goes for a home that is well planned and doesn't waste space to circulation, or has a kitchen with views into a living room so you can chat with friends and family when you are cooking, or allows cross flows of air to cool it in the summer. None of these things cost more, but they will give you a lot more pleasure and enjoyment out of your home.

HOUSING TYPES

There are many different types of home, from a family home to a mobile home, a mansion block to a tower block, detached or semi-detached. The types included on these pages are in no way a definitive list. Types, after all, are end products rather than starting points and they are constantly evolving. Think, for example, about the way in which Victorian warehouses are now being converted into loft apartments. Or the introduction of live/work housing that reflects the changing nature of our working and living habits in the twenty-first century. The introduction of new technology enables us to question, challenge and evolve new types of housing.

Town houses

Historically town houses defined the character of market towns. They were also well suited to families who liked the convenience of urban living. The town house could be considered a hybrid of the terrace and semi-detached, and is likely to have a least one party wall – that is a shared wall with a neighbour – though it may be adjoined on both sides. It will probably have three or four storeys, or maybe even five if the attic is also habitable, giving the town house a flexible layout for the competing demands of the family, entertaining and work.

Town houses have a degree of individuality without upsetting the collective order of a city street or square and are architecturally distinct and varied, so they won't be as uniform as terraced houses. They also, often, have compact gardens which, if well designed and enclosed, provide great additional living space for outdoor eating or practicing your golf swing.

Type

Describing buildings by type helps us to recognise a superstore from a hospital or train station. 'Type' refers both to the use of a building and to the formal expression of that use.

While some building types have had a bad press, the reality is that there is no such thing as a bad housing type. Any housing type can be well designed. And if it is also well maintained, then it will be a delightful place to live.

Not all homes can be necessarily categorised as a particular type.

Terraced – average 75-150 houses per *hectare*

The terraced house characterised the eighteenth century. The historian Sigfried Gideon cited Bloomsbury with its terraces arranged in streets and squares as a high point of urban development. Another architectural historian Steen Eiler Rasmussen reflected on its suitability to the lifestyles of the day, stating, "The English have cultivated everything connected with daily life." The terraced house model was flexible, adaptable and affordable.

Semi-detached – average 30-50 houses per *hectare*

The semi-detached house characterised the twentieth century, epitomising the idea of a suburban utopia, a compromise between the attractions of the detached house and the economies of construction evident in terraced houses. The semi-detached house can easily accommodate an informal living style and take on the creativity of its owners through the application of extensions and decoration. It combines the ideals of light, space and access to the outdoors.

Detached – average 10-20 houses per *hectare*

The detached house embraces both the historic country house as well as the late twentieth century housing estate. The detached house represents a desire for individuality and isolation. It is generally assumed that most people want a detached house. However, in 1911 only 10 per cent of dwellings in England and Wales were detached or semi-detached. The development of public transport and the growth of the suburbs increased this after the First World War. In 1993 detached houses accounted for 44 per cent of new mortgages. Architects such as Edwin Lutyens, Le Corbusier and Mies van der Rohe have designed some of the finest examples of detached family houses.

Courtyard house – average 30-75 houses per *hectare*

Arguably more popular overseas, the courtyard house celebrates the relationship of indoor space with garden space. There are some excellent examples in this country from the 1960s to the present by architects such as Aldington and Craig or PRP who designed courtyard houses at the 'Millennium village of the future' of 1963 in Hatfield. Here living space looks onto an enclosed landscaped courtyard offering a protected garden with a high degree of privacy.

Mansion blocks – average 150-300 dwellings per *hectare*

These are often set around a communal square or garden for use by residents and can accommodate apartments and maisonettes. The classic mansion block typically accommodated shops on the ground floor, offices on the first, affluent apartments on middle floors and 'affordable' housing in the attic. The contemporary mansion block has evolved, so that it more typically accommodates expensive penthouses at its top.

Deck access blocks – average 150+ dwellings per *hectare*

In 1848 the Society for Improving the Condition of the Labouring Classes proposed plans for neat, well built dwellings. One model featured flats entered off walkways either side of a shared staircase, and this became known as deck access. This model didn't gain real popularity until the 1950s when the walkways became known as 'streets in the sky', places where residents could sit outside, while their children played safely. One example is the Park Hill estate in Sheffield where the decks are wide enough for a milk float and rubbish trolley to circulate. Many were stereotyped as housing that should never be repeated but there are recent successful examples at Chorlton Park in Manchester and Raines Dairy in Stoke Newington, London.

Raines Dairy, London

Tower blocks – average 200+ dwellings per *hectare*

The end of the nineteenth century saw the invention of the elevator and, thanks to the growing use of steel in construction, the birth of the skyscraper. It became viable to build over five storeys, initially for warehouses and offices, and later residential towers. The popularity of well-managed tower blocks such as the Barbican and the refurbished Trellick Tower (both in London) has sparked a renewed interest in residential towers. The importance of good management – in these cases, seen in the presence of an on-site concierge – can mean the difference between success and failure.

Split level blocks – average 150+ dwellings per *hectare*

This ingenious housing type was developed by the architect Le Corbusier in his 'Unité d'Habitation' scheme. It provides apartments split over two levels and interlocked around a central access corridor. These arrangements allowed each maisonette to have a double height living space and views from both sides of the building. A recent example of split level apartments can be seen at Timber Wharf in Manchester.

Did you know?

The average fabric heat loss (that is, heat lost through walls, windows, doors and roof) in a block of nine city apartments is 40 per cent less than equivalent sized detached dwellings.

HOUSING STYLE

Vernacular

Vernacular is a term that refers to buildings whose form and use of materials is regionally distinct. So, we can recognise buildings in the Cotswolds because of the type of stone they use, and the familiarity of steeply pitched roofs found across the Fens.

Construction techniques are now more streamlined and efficient, with the same components being used in homes that are being built as far apart as Kent and Northumberland.

As a result today's architecture is no longer so specific to a particular region. Standard building types can, however, be modified by incorporating architectural symbols particular to the area, whether these be the pitch of a roof, the choice of timber weatherboarding or the use of a certain kind of brick or stone.

Good design and good taste are two different things. Good taste is a matter of opinion whereas good design is about how well things work. It is about a design solution that has been well executed. And while it might not suit everyone's taste, it will, nonetheless, still merit the description, 'good design'.

Your preference for a particular style will reflect your aspirations, memories and cultural baggage. Architects rarely talk about their buildings in terms of a specific style, because style tends to be a label given to a building after it has been built. More often than not, a style is associated with a particular era, for example, Victorian, Georgian or Regency. This helps us to both picture the sort of building that we might be interested in buying, as well as how old it is likely to be.

Just like fashion or car design, housing styles change over time, albeit somewhat more slowly. This is because it takes longer for the factors that influence housing design to change, whether these be construction technology or lifestyles. Consequently, it would be pointless to simply copy the styles of yesteryear. Our references are now broader and our needs and expectations have changed fundamentally.

One myth here that is worth dispelling is the notion that symmetry equals good, and asymmetry bad. Symmetry isn't necessarily more pleasing to the eye – chaos can be as fascinating as order, for instance. A building doesn't need to be symmetrical to look good. In fact, the closer the relationship between its internal organisation of space and the design of its *elevations*, the less likely it is to be symmetrical.

Classical architecture, for example, has highly ordered *elevations* which dictate the arrangement and design of the space within. Organic architecture on the other hand lets the use of the space and the layout of the interior determine what the *elevations* will look like.

Gob-ons

When symbols or characteristics of vernacular are superficially applied, they are called '*gob-ons*' by developers (the term is indicative of the esteem in which they are held by the building industry). A *gob-on* might include a fibreglass chimney stack which doesn't connect to a fireplace, but is purely there for effect. Another popular *gob-on* is applied timber beams, intended to suggest an Elizabethan cottage. Others include columns pretending to be the grand portico of a classical country house, decorative coach house doors, wagon wheels and carriage lamps.

HOUSE BUILDING ESSENTIALS

A sustainable house will be durable, versatile and energy efficient, that is it will be long life, loose fit and low energy.

Long life

Whether made of bricks, wood, steel or concrete – or, more likely, a mixture of all four – we expect our homes to last at least for our lifetime. After all, surviving Greek temples are proof of the durability of stone and block construction. The oldest surviving timber framed buildings date from the thirteenth century (although we are more familiar with the timber frame barns and cottages of the sixteenth and seventeenth centuries). Benyon and Marshall's flax mill in Shrewsbury, the oldest surviving steel framed building, was constructed at the end of the eighteenth century. And although concrete was invented by the Romans, the earliest successful use of reinforced concrete can be seen in the Steinerhaus in Vienna, built in 1911.

Today's homes are more likely to be built, or at least part built, in a factory. While traditional brick construction still has to contend with the hazards of a muddy field and exposure to the elements, frame construction can be engineered within the warmth and security of a factory. This type of construction also has additional benefits, such as quality control, and less material waste. A building made using frame construction also frees up what can be done with the walls – they can be made entirely from glass or packed with insulation.

Building a home off-site is not new – since the early thirteenth century, timber frame buildings have been prefabricated, because of the need to cut and fit joints before works could begin. Today a home might use factory produced roof trusses and windows, combined with flat packed timber or steel frame walls and floors or even fully prefabricated bathroom and kitchen pods, with factory-installed tiles and fittings. And all this can result in a home as durable as anything that has been built over the previous centuries.

Off the shelf

In Finland, more than half the population live in factory produced homes.

NHBC

Check that your builder is registered with the National House Building Council (NHBC). Only builders and developers who can demonstrate financial security and technical competence can register with the NHBC. This means that they must follow NHBC Rules and build homes according to NHBC Standards of construction.

Acoustics

It is a government requirement that new homes should meet a certain *acoustic* standard to prevent noise transfer between properties. A new home will either have been tested to demonstrate that it meets these standards or will use standard construction methods that have been approved by the local building inspector.

Brick construction is still the most common method of building in the UK.

These houses are built using a highly insulated flat-packed timber frame which can be externally finished in any material, such as brickwork or timber weatherboarding.

WHAT TO ASK

→ How is the property built and are the materials used expensive to maintain.

→ Has the property used sustainable construction techniques and materials from renewable sources.

→ Has the property passed acoustic testing.

→ Does the wall construction limit the possibility of hanging pictures, hooks or shelves.

WHAT TO LOOK FOR

→ Internal walls sufficient for reducing sound transfer between internal rooms.

Murray Grove, London

Murray Grove was built using some of the most advanced construction techniques currently available. Entire rooms were precision engineered and fabricated in a factory. These were then delivered to the site on the back of a lorry and were put together within a matter of days. Timber and terracotta cladding, balconies and stairs were then added on site.

Party walls

The Party Wall Act ensures that reasonable works can proceed without undue obstruction from your neighbours. A party wall surveyor will help negotiations with your neighbours, monitoring the impact that the works have on their property. For instance, if you are planning to build a conservatory, with one wall sitting on your neighbour's boundary, you may need to take down their garden fence and dig up part of their patio. A party wall surveyor will agree any compensation and remedial works due in fairness to both parties.

Air quality

Research shows that people spend 90 per cent of their time in buildings so it's worth knowing that the indoor air quality of your new home will be as safe as possible. Ask if the builder has taken steps to avoid the use of harmful toxic substances, for example by using low *VOC* (volatile organic compound) paint.

Loose fit

Traditionally, plans or estate agent's details will label rooms in a conventional manner: the living room, bedroom one, bedroom two, the bathroom, and so on. This tends to fix our perception of a space, even before we have seen a property. It can also predetermine how we might use our home in the future, inhibiting flexibility and change. So, instead of looking at the rooms in the traditional way, try to think about the versatility of their space. In other words, don't ask 'How many?', think 'How versatile?'.

Can rooms be put to a variety of uses? Are the living and dining rooms interchangeable? Can a bedroom become a study? Can the front room become an office? Is there room in the garage for a work bench or bench press as well as your car? A well-designed home can accommodate our changing demands and lifestyles by providing flexible and cost effective layouts.

On average, people move home every seven years. Most of us would probably prefer to be able to adapt our homes, rather than face the prospect of another stressful move. So the next question you need to ask is, 'Is the property ACE?'– or, in other words, can you Add, Convert and Extend?

Adding a new bathroom, utility room or even just additional appliances will depend on the positioning of your drainpipes and water pipes. Similarly, it will be easier – and more cost effective – to place a new ground floor bathroom directly underneath the first floor bathroom, rather than on the other side of the house. If you need to add a disabled toilet, you will need at least 3.5sqm additional space, in order to accommodate a wheelchair's turning circle.

Your ability to convert a property depends on its construction, as well as on the position of its services. If the external walls are load-bearing – that is, they carry the weight of the property – then you will have more freedom in how you configure the rooms inside. If you have internal load-bearing walls, however, you will need to seek advice from an architect or engineer, and your options to convert will then depend on their advice, *Building regulations* and planning permission.

Planning restrictions, as well as any *covenants* on the building will also affect your ability to extend your home. If the building is listed you will need listed building consent. And if you are in a conservation area, then planning permission will be needed for what might appear to be apparently cosmetic changes.

It is best to seek advice from your local authority planning department – if you fail to obtain planning permission for any building works, you might have to take them down at a later date.

Whether you are adding, converting or extending, your works will need to meet the requirements of the local authority building inspector, so it is always wise to seek professional advice to ensure that they meet the regulations. In addition, if your property adjoins another – if you live in a semi-detached or terraced house, for example – then you will need a Party Wall Agreement, if the works are likely to impact on the wall that you share with your neighbour. Again, it is best to seek professional advice about a Party Wall Agreement, both to ease the process and as a means of mediation between neighbours.

Building regulations

Building regulations (regs) are there to ensure the safety of people occupying a building, as well as adjoining buildings. The regulations cover a range of issues, including fire protection, means of escape, drainage, energy conservation, structural requirements and disabled access requirements.

This proposal in Seedley and Langworthy, Manchester, shows how typical back-to-back terraced housing can be adapted to suit modern lifestyles. The back walls are replaced with floor to ceiling glazing, the living room moves to the first floor and the roof space is opened up to allow in more light. The relatively small backyards are joined together to create a communal garden.

Architects

Architects are regulated professionals who, as well as offering design services, can manage the planning application process on your behalf, advise you on the requirements of *Building regulations* and deal with your builders. In the UK, the title, 'Architect' is protected by an Act of Parliament, so anyone presenting themselves as an architect must be registered with the Architects Registration Board (ARB), and is subject to their code of conduct. The Architects Registration Board and the Royal Institute of British Architects (RIBA) can provide you with contact details of architects in your area.

The HangerHouse™ concept house suggests an idea of the future of flexible living and how developers might come to offer lifetime service. The house uses a framework from which the home owner can 'hang' the house of their choice. The owner can order whatever add-ons or configurations they desire from a wide selection of ready-made rooms and exterior finishes, whilst The HangerHouse Company would be on call to add, convert or extend the HangerHouse™ as lifestyles and circumstances change – a one stop shop for all the home owner's needs.

A roof extension or loft conversion will require planning permission, check with your local authority.

WHAT TO ASK	WHAT TO LOOK FOR
→ Is there potential to convert the loft into another room.	→ The layout should be adaptable for future lifestyle changes.
→ Which internal walls are structural.	→ The doors should be wide enough for a wheelchair.
→ Are there any planning restrictions.	→ Think about how an extension might impact on your garden – and your neighbour's.
→ Is the property in a conservation area and is this likely to affect any future plans to extend.	→ A south facing garden is the ideal location if you want to add a conservatory.
	→ Is the roof pitch and structure suitable for a future loft conversion.

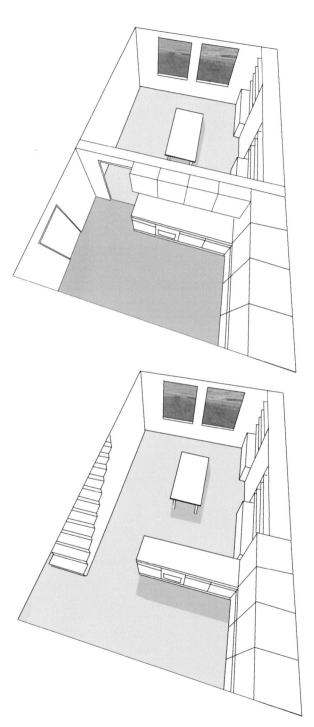

Opening up your space

If internal walls are non-structural – in other words, they are not supporting the floor or roof above – then removing them can be relatively straightforward.

If they are structural, then you will need to seek the advice of a structural engineer before you remove them. You will also need to install additional structural support and get building approval from your local authority before commencing the works.

A ground floor conservatory or rear extension may be categorised as 'permitted development' for which you will need a license from your local authority.

Low energy

Is your home lightweight or heavyweight? While this might appear to be a flippant question – you are unlikely to be able to weigh your house, after all – it will affect the *energy efficiency* of your home. A heavyweight property will typically be constructed of blockwork and brickwork walls, with insulation between these two layers of material. It will retain heat longer, but will take longer to heat up – which is good if you are at home most of the time.

A lightweight property, on the other hand, will typically be constructed using a timber or steel frame. The areas between the supporting frame structure can be packed with insulation and covered in any material, whether brick, tiles or timber. The advantage of a lightweight property is that it will be very quick to heat up. The disadvantage is that it will cool down fast.

Energy efficiency should be taken for granted in newly built homes. Indeed, some homes can be so energy efficient that they can be kept warm just by using body heat. While it is unlikely that you will be looking at a property with this level of insulation, you should be asking the seller or developer about the *energy efficiency* of your potential new home.

The internal layout of the property will also have implications for *energy efficiency*. Ideally, utility spaces should act as buffer zones to the north, with living spaces being located to the south of the property.

EcoHomes standard

Homes which meet the Building Research Establishment's 'EcoHomes' Very Good or Excellent standard have a significantly reduced impact on the environment. The EcoHomes scheme is a voluntary accreditation scheme that builders can use to demonstrate that they are building homes that are more environmentally friendly. This means they are likely to be more energy and water efficient than standard homes and so save you money – and protect the environment.

These thermal images show that the home on the left has a well insulated roof but poorly insulated walls. The properties on the right have well insulated walls, with heat loss showing only around the doors and windows.

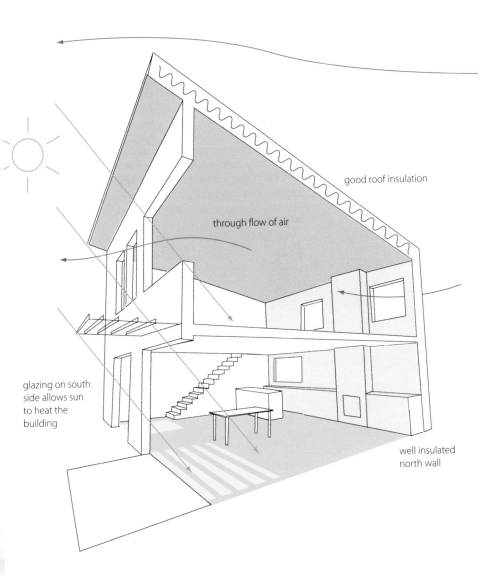

good roof insulation

through flow of air

glazing on south side allows sun to heat the building

well insulated north wall

In this illustration the prevailing wind creates positive pressure on one side of the house and negative pressure on the side away from the wind direction. The change of pressure helps cross ventilation.

An apartment that only faces one way or only has windows on one side – called single *aspect* – will have poorer air quality and less chance of a cross flow of air. And because warm air rises, a rooflight positioned above a staircase, for example, can help draw air up through a home.

Insulation

Heat rises so the most important place for good insulation in a home is in the roof, followed by the walls. Increasingly, new houses are also including insulation under the ground floor slab to prevent heat being lost to the cold ground below.

When you are calculating the cost of your new home, you should bear its *energy efficiency* in mind. You might have calculated your monthly outgoings on the basis of mortgage repayments, council tax, service charges and insurance, but the *energy efficiency* of your home could save you up to £1,000 a year. It will also go some way in helping to save the environment as well. It is worth knowing what the SAP rating or Carbon Index is.

SAP rating

A Standard Assessment Procedure (*SAP*) rating, based on typical usage of heating and hot water, will result in a figure between 1 and 120 that can be equated to actual yearly running costs.

Carbon Index

Using the same data, a *carbon Index* figure, which indicates the level of carbon emissions from the home from 1 (bad) to 10 (good), can also be produced.

SAP rating

yearly space and water heating costs (£)

carbon index

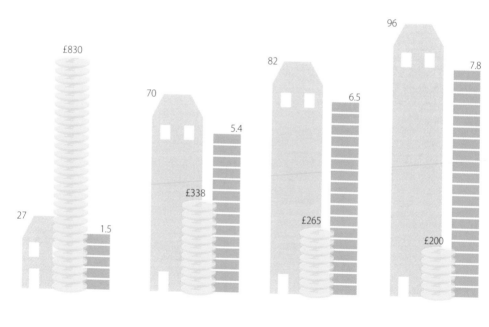

1900 property as constructed with gas central heating fitted 20 years ago	1900 property with insulation improvements and condensing gas central heating	New-build pre April 2002, with condensing gas central heating	New-build post April 2002, with condensing gas central heating

The chart shows that running costs reduced as a house becomes more energy efficient.

BedZed, Sutton

This innovative landmark housing scheme brings all the current ideas about environmentally conscious living together in one place, including photovoltaics, *sun space*s to absorb solar heat, grass roofs, and a combined heat and power system fuelled by woodchips. The development includes family housing, apartments, *live/work units*, a medical centre, nursery, café, sports pitch and clubhouse. It is carbon neutral, which means it doesn't add to the atmosphere's carbon dioxide levels and any energy used during construction has been negated by positive environmental benefits, such as tree planting and recycling. Energy demands have been reduced to 25 per cent of a conventional home of a similar size. All buildings at BedZed are low allergen construction, avoiding substances such as formaldehyde, which has been associated with sick building syndrome. Grey water – that is, any water that has been used in the home, except water from toilets – is cleaned and filtered on site.

WHAT TO ASK

→ How are the walls and roof constructed and are they well insulated.

→ What is the *insulation rating* and *energy efficiency* of the new property. You may be able to get an EcoHomes rating.

→ Does the property have any special energy saving features for example, *condensing gas boiler*, double- or triple- glazing.

→ Has the builder used materials that have a low environmental impact, such as timber from an independently certified, well managed source.

WHAT TO LOOK FOR

→ A draught lobby to exterior doors or buffer spaces that will reduce heat loss from living spaces.

→ Utility spaces or less occupied rooms to the north will reduce heat loss.

→ *Sun space*s to the south will maximise heat gain.

→ Heating that can be separately controlled in different parts of the home.

→ Are low energy lighting and appliances installed. New appliances should have the *Energy Efficiency* Recommended logo.

→ Make sure that the windows and doors avoid energy inefficient materials such as *UPVC*.

SPACE AND LAYOUT

The way in which we view our homes is largely based on the Victorian model. Before that, rooms weren't defined by their use – living, dining or bedroom, for example. Neither were they separated from each other by corridors, stairs and hallways. In the sixteenth century, most rooms had two doors, providing links to other rooms, creating a network of interconnected rooms, like the squares on a chessboard.

A hundred years later, corridors were introduced, essentially as a way of keeping servants out of sight of the ladies and gentlemen of the house. By the Victorian era, most rooms only had one door, thereby necessitating the rearrangement of the home to incorporate corridors and enclosed staircases. These became the spine of the home, off of which hung each room.

Such an arrangement, it was believed, reduced the likelihood of a chance encounter. Alexander Klein took this theory to the extreme with the creation in 1928 of 'The Functional House for Frictionless Living', which he designed to ensure that the occupants never crossed paths as they moved around the house.

In the twenty-first century, our notion of privacy is still derived from this Victorian model and the majority of homes in the UK still follow this formula. Few of us, however, live like Victorians. Gradually homes are being built that challenge us to think of spaces instead of rooms. Open plan and loft style layouts suit some lifestyles and are becoming increasingly common. In this way, we might be able to leave another Victorian legacy behind us.

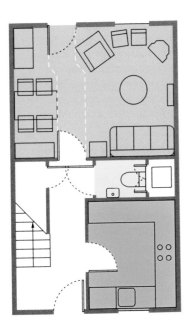
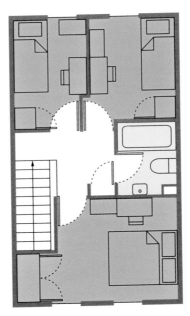

A tight space

The layout of your home will have a noticeable impact on your lifestyle.

The plans above, from a typical developer, are for a house designed for a family of four. The internal layout is based on the Victorian model with, for example, a kitchen designed for an age when women were expected to cook behind closed doors. In the twenty-first century, we'd probably prefer to be able to supervise our children or chat to our dinner guests while cooking. Each room has been designed to a standard size. It is so tightly planned that there is no room for a clothes horse or anything other than standard sized furniture. As a result, people who wish to individualise such a home will find it difficult to incorporate non-standard items – whether an oversize sofa or a Welsh dresser. This model offers minimum built-in storage and the kitchen is impractically separated from the dining area by two doors and a corridor.

living

bedroom

kitchen

bathroom

The only way you will know if you are getting value for money is to know how much space you are being offered.

It is an unfortunate fact that homes are getting smaller. The average size of homes built in England between 1980 and 2000 was 10 per cent smaller than those built before 1980. Don't, however, give up on the idea of buying a new-build house – if you are armed with the right information, and ask the right questions, you should be able to determine whether what you are buying is worth your life's savings.

One way of working out the value of the property is to divide its price by the size of its floor area. This will give you a price per square metre that you can then compare with other properties. Check whether the area you are being quoted is 'net' or 'gross', as there is a big difference. The gross floor area is the total footprint including walls. Net floor area excludes walls, and is a measure of the total usable space. The way in which the walls enclose a room will affect how you feel about its space. An open plan design, for example, can make things seem more spacious. Think about your lifestyle. An open plan will work for small family sizes, but may drive big families mad especially if the property is small. Corridors or staircases may or may not be included in the area measurement so you need to check this as it will affect the amount of remaining liveable space.

These images clearly show how ceiling heights have lowered and window sizes have got smaller over the last 50 years. As a result room sizes have shrunk and the quality of light has diminished.

WHAT TO ASK

→ What is the total net floor area of the property.

→ What is the total gross floor area of the property.

→ Does the property comply with *building regulations* for fire enclosure and means of escape.

WHAT TO LOOK FOR

→ Rooms should allow different configurations of furniture.

→ You should be able to fit a desk, a bed and a wardrobe into any potential study-bedroom.

→ Can you see between rooms, for example, from the kitchen to the dining room.

→ Doorways, corridors and openings should be large enough for you to get your furniture to where you want it.

Think about what kind of layout will suit your lifestyle. The plans below show comparisons of apartments of a similar size with the same number of bedrooms. The degree of enclosure will affect the quality and your perception of space. An open plan may be more space efficient and feel more open but, perhaps, offer less privacy. A cellular plan may result in wasted corridor space but allow you to close off the kitchen from the living area, for example.

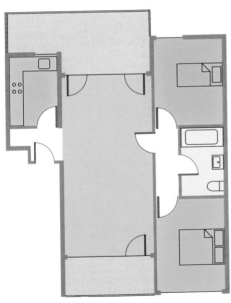

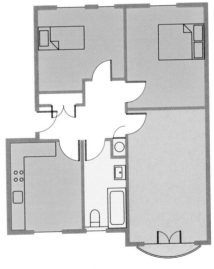

living

bedroom

kitchen

bathroom

balcony

Open plan
2 bedroom, 4 person, 74sqm
- separate kitchen enclosure but isolated from dining space
- double *aspect* living room
- small kitchen but living space big enough for dining area
- natural light and views from entrance
- large balcony for outside dining

Cellular plan
2 bedroom, 4 person, 72sqm
- deep plan living room with single *aspect*
- kitchen has space for table and chairs
- unlit enclosed hallway on arrival
- balcony with space for pot plant

You should also think about the effect ceiling heights have on the quality of space. The basic rule of thumb is that the larger the room, the higher the ceiling needs to be in order to maintain proportions, otherwise, it may feel claustrophobic. The generally acceptable ceiling height for bedrooms is 2.4 metres. Living rooms, often have higher ceilings – for example, Edwardian and Georgian houses often have living rooms with ceiling heights between 2.8 and 3.2 metres.

Then there is the question of how much space you need. The generally-accepted amount of space per person standard was set out in the Parker Morris report of 1961, following research commissioned by the government of the day into concerns about overcrowding. These mandatory standards – some of which can be seen in the illustration below – were abolished in the 1980s and, as a consequence, space standards have begun to shrink again.

Take, for example, the trend for 'microflats'. Some of these are as small as 33sqm and, if occupied by two people, are almost a third below the Parker Morris standard of 44.5sqm. Having said that, however, some builders are now working to the Parker Morris Standard plus 10 per cent.

It is important to insist on finding out the floor area of your new home. Knowing the number of bedrooms isn't enough: a three bed house built in the 1930s, for example, can be up to 30 per cent larger than a three bed house built in the 1990s. And only through knowing the total floor area will you really be able to work out whether you are getting true value for money.

Show homes

Show homes have a sneaky habit of not always being what they appear. They may be styled by the latest TV celebrity makeover artist and look impressive, but make sure you look below the surface. A standard trick adopted in many show homes is leaving doors off frames to give the impression that rooms will be larger than they are. If you overlook this, you might find that once you have moved your furniture in, you can't open the door. Show homes built at 'Home Show Exhibitions' are often built 10 per cent bigger than the real thing. This might ease the movement of thousands of visitors at the exhibition, but it won't truly reflect what you will get when the home is built.

Table of Parker Morris space standards

Net floor area of habitable accommodations (sqm)

Number of people	6	5	4	3	2	1
Apartment	86.5	79.0	70.0	57.0	44.5	30.0
Semi-detached	92.5	82.0	72.0			
Three storey house	98.0	98.0				

Internal Storage space (sqm)

Number of people	6	5	4	3	2	1
Houses	4.5	4.5	4.5	4.0	4.0	3.0
Apartments and maisonettes	3.5	3.5	3.5	3.0	3.0	2.5

Source: New Metric Handbook, Patricia Tutt and David Adler

Value for money

The table below gives you an idea of the true value of three different homes – A, B and C. It is assumed that each is on the market for £200,000, and all benefit from being located on the same street (i.e. each has the same quality of light and access to neighbourhood amenities, etc.) As the properties are of different ages they will have different running costs. The formula therefore, rather than just dividing price by floor area, calculates their relative values including running and maintenance costs.

	Price	Floor area	Energy cost (over 10 years)[1]	Maintenance costs (first ten years)[2]	Cumulative cost (cost price + energy cost + maintenance cost)	Value for money (£ per sqm)
A	£200,000	104sqm	£3,380	£40,000	£243,380	£2,340
B	£200,000	80sqm	£2,000	0	£202,000	£2,535
C	£200,000	104sqm	£2,000	0	£202,000	£1,942

[1] refer to table on page 100, [2] where maintenance = 2 per cent of sales value for a period property

Property A: Built in 1900, is 104sqm, costs £4,000 a year to maintain (based on estate agents lore that the maintenance cost of a period property is 2 per cent of its sales value per annum) and has a carbon rating of 5.4 (refer to table on page 100).

Property B: Built in 2002, is 80sqm, with no annual maintenance costs and annual energy costs of £200.

Property C: Also built in 2002, is 204sqm, with no annual maintenance costs and annual energy costs of £200.

Property C represents the best value for money, because it has been built to premium space standards. The period property, meanwhile, is better value than the smaller newly built home, even though it costs more to run.

How much space do you need for your family?

KITCHENS

A property will outlive the fittings and furnishings it contains so identifying whether a home is well built and has a successful flexible layout should be your priority. On average, kitchen fittings are replaced anything upwards of five times during the life of a home. Nonetheless, it is worth assessing the design merits of this regularly used room – the better planned it is, the better long term value you will get out of it.

Do you consider cooking a spectator sport or do you prefer to cook alone? Is it a pleasure, or a chore? If you prefer an enclosed kitchen, away from prying eyes and critical comments, you will need to think about the relationship between the kitchen and its adjacent rooms. Can you look through to them? Or will your cry for assistance necessitate a walk down a corridor? If your kitchen is also a family room, does it need a relationship to the garden if you enjoy dining al fresco?

When assessing the design of your kitchen, think about its three principle functions: food storage, preparation and cooking. There should be enough storage so that you can separate out dry foods from perishables or crockery from utensils, and there should be a variety of storage on offer: cupboards, drawers, open shelves and racks.

In preparing and cooking food, studies show that a working triangle between the three main activity zones – the cooker, sink and fridge – will be the most *ergonomic*. Make sure that there is adequate space between each of these appliances.

Generally, good kitchen design is a matter of common sense. Sinks tend to be situated in front of a window, to give you a view into the garden or street and make you feel less claustrophobic when you are washing up or peeling the spuds. A gas hob can't go in front of a window because this will make it difficult to see whether it is lit.

Think about other activities that might happen in a kitchen. If, for example, you haven't got a utility room and your kitchen is open plan, then the noise of a washing machine in mid-cycle while you're having a meal will not add to your quality of life. Look, instead, for an opportunity to isolate the washing machine in a tall cupboard, with space above it for a laundry basket or to dry clothes.

WHAT TO LOOK FOR

→ Adequate sockets for appliances, but none directly near a water source – i.e. the sink.

→ Accessible electrical switches for the cooker, fridge and washing machine.

→ Space for a dishwasher.

→ Space for the disposal of rubbish and recycling organic and inorganic waste.

→ Clearance for cupboard doors, with no clashes between cupboard doors or cupboard and room doors.

→ Good lighting to avoid overshadowing.

→ Easy to clean surfaces.

→ An extractor fan, or even a heat recovery unit above the cooker.

When you view a home, try mentally preparing a meal, thinking about where you would store the vegetables, if there are adequate work surfaces to chop them up and how near the sink is when you need to drain them. Such an exercise will help you to test whether the kitchen is going to be fit for its intended purpose.

BATHROOMS

Archimedes famously had his best ideas in the bath. And, in a parody that reflects many male user habits, Rodin's 'The Thinker' is often displayed sitting on the toilet. If we considered the bathroom as not just a place to wash, but also to muse, we get much better value out of this much overlooked room.

Would a view of the sky or of nature improve the quality of your bathing? Would task lighting and shelving help you if you want to read in the bath or on the toilet? On a more practical level, if you are buying a family home do you need an additional WC separate to the bathroom to avoid bottlenecks at busy times of the day? You might want to think about *acoustic* issues, whether to avoid embarrassing noises being heard by your neighbours or to improve your attempts at singing in the shower. And you will need to check that the bathroom is well ventilated and heated, to avoid condensation – and the resulting mould.

A well planned bathroom isn't complicated. Of course, you will need to decide on your needs – a bath or shower, sink, WC and maybe even a bidet. But what is more important is to think about the space around these items, as well as what your needs will be if your circumstances change. A well designed bathroom, for example, will allow space to bath and change a baby or for disabled access. It will also have a medicine cabinet out of the reach of children and a sink positioned to give you adequate elbow room. For health and safety reasons, you can't have electric sockets in bathrooms, but a shaver socket will probably be desirable and is often incorporated into over-sink lighting. You will probably also want to make sure that the light is suitable for those early morning shaves or those quick applications of make-up before going out for the night.

The energy and water efficiency of your bathroom is important to bear in mind too, especially if your water supply is metered. Showers are more efficient than baths – in fact you can have three showers for the price of one bath. Wet rooms – where the room is fully tiled and water goes down a floor drain – offer a fantastic opportunity to do away with shower trays or screens. It is worth checking that the floors have an adequate fall to drain properly, so do not be afraid to run the shower when you are viewing a property. The installation of low or dual flush WCs, as well as efficient taps and showers will save you money without any reduction in performance. And if there are grey water recycling facilities available – where all water that has been used in the home (excepting toilet water) is recycled – then your water bill will be even further reduced.

WHAT TO ASK

→ An adequate hot water supply to suit your family bathing habits and times.

→ Access to services, such as a cistern for repair and inspection.

→ The location of the overflow from storage tanks and cisterns (water should be stopped if it overflows as it will damage the fabric of the building).

→ A water efficient WC.

WHAT TO LOOK FOR

→ A non-slip floor.

→ Adequate leg room in front of the WC and bidet.

→ Adequate water pressure for a shower or bath.

→ Enough heated drying and hanging space for towels.

→ Space for a medicine cabinet or shelf near the sink.

→ Mechanical ventilation in the form of an extractor fan to remove moist air.

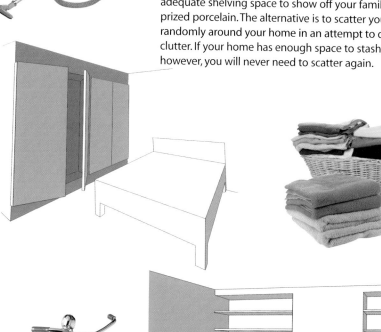

STORAGE

What do the following have in common: ironing board, laundry basket, prams, vacuum cleaner, toys, skateboards, bicycles, holiday gear, suitcases?

The chances are that none of them will be on display when you visit a show home. And yet they – and many other objects – are likely to be found in most homes. In fact, you will probably need around 22 per cent of the floor area of your new home in which to accommodate all those 'not being used at the moment, but they will be used at some stage in the future' objects.

Now one option is to have a car boot sale every month or so, thereby religiously clearing away the clutter in your life. Another, more realistic option, is to make sure that your new home has enough storage space. In a well-designed home this will include built-in storage, in which you can stash away unwanted presents or toolboxes. It should also have adequate shelving space to show off your family photos or prized porcelain. The alternative is to scatter your possessions randomly around your home in an attempt to disguise the clutter. If your home has enough space to stash and show, however, you will never need to scatter again.

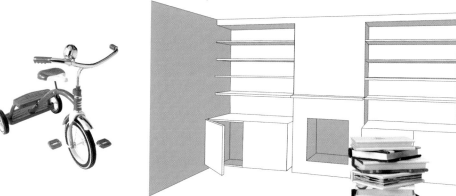

WHAT TO ASK

→ 'Can you put that away' – whatever 'it' is, ask yourself whether you will be able to in your new home.

→ Which walls will be able to support shelving or extra cupboards.

→ Can the attic floor support heavy items. Does the design of the trusses restrict access.

WHAT TO LOOK FOR

→ An attic with easy and safe access.

→ Built-in storage in bedrooms, the kitchen and hallway.

→ An airing cupboard for laundry.

Take it away

If everything about the house or apartment that you are considering buying is perfect apart from the lack of storage space, then you might want to consider the self-storage option. You won't be alone. Between 1994 and 2004, the number of self-storage warehouses in the UK has exploded, from 30 to over 300. Whether it is your old collection of vinyl or suitcases full of memorabilia that you can't bear to part with, self-storage units give you a relatively cheap means of maintaining a minimalist lifestyle.

LIGHT

The importance of the lighting in your home should not be underestimated. It can make a room feel warm or cool, dramatic or dull. It will impact on the intensity of the colour scheme, as well as the textures and feel of the space. In essence, light can make or break a home.

Natural light

Between 1696 and 1851, home owners had to pay a tax on the number of windows in their houses, a tax that was only abolished when officials realised that homes were being built with intolerably few windows. In the twenty-first century, the number of windows in our homes is neither constrained by direct taxation nor, thanks to the development of double-glazing and insulation technology, by concerns over heat loss. Generally, it is better to have more windows, rather than too few. And it is easier to shut out excess light or make a space more private with curtains or blinds than to knock a hole in your front wall in order to let light in.

Some homes may contain rooms without external windows, such as corridors or bathrooms. One way to overcome the lack of natural light is to borrow light from other rooms, by having clear or frosted panels between rooms or incorporated into doors. This helps you to make the most of your natural light, and not to become over reliant on artificial light sources.

Windows are, however, not just about light. Windows are as much for ventilation as lighting. Modern building standards mean new homes are a lot more airtight and so waste less energy. Typically, there is a lot of moisture in a home – particularly with newly built homes – which will cause condensation if not properly dealt with. Condensation occurs when moist air meets cold surfaces. Good ventilation and heating will help overcome condensation, which if left unchecked will lead to the growth of mould. Modern window systems have *trickle vents* which should be kept open to help reduce condensation whilst an extractor fan in a bathroom and kitchen will help combat the same problem in these rooms. And homes that have windows on both sides are better for cross ventilation than those that only face one way.

Bay windows allow more light to enter a room and give a greater feeling of space.

Large windows and French doors allow light to flood in and connect inside and outside spaces.

Glazing in a conservatory and lower ground floor or basement extension allows natural light into otherwise dark rooms.

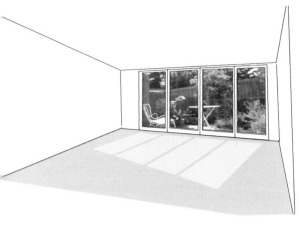

A fully glazed wall

A room where a whole wall is glazed will offer plenty of light that changes throughout the day. The light will be much brighter than in enclosed rooms and reach deep into the room. In addition, extensive glazing can help in visually connecting a home with its garden.

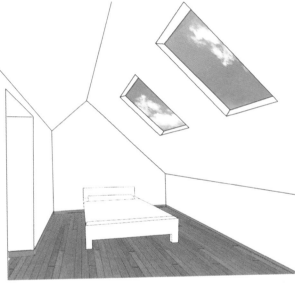

A rooflight

This offers the opportunity to light all parts of the room. As well as providing even lighting across a room during the daytime, a rooflight will give you a view of the stars at night.

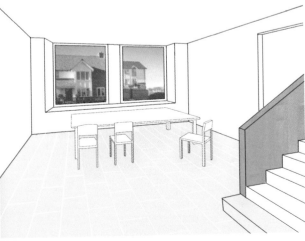

Windows on one side

Rooms lit from one side are typical in most houses in the UK. Windows on the long side of a room will help ensure an even distribution of light. A narrow deep room with a window at one end will have poor natural light and may well create glare. Additional windows in adjacent walls or on the opposite side of the room will help reduce glare.

Artificial light

Changing the artificial lighting is one of the easiest ways to alter the mood and feel of your home. Whether you use spot lights, standard lamps or desk lamps, artificial lighting plays a critical role in the way we enjoy our homes. So when you are searching for a new home, it is worth checking the number of power points and ceiling lights, as well as where they are positioned.

A central pendant light in the middle of each room is unlikely to be sufficient for the complexity of tasks and atmospheres that we have come to expect in a modern home. Good lighting will ease a variety of everyday tasks, whether these be shaving, washing up or cooking. Well positioned, *ergonomic* artificial lighting can make a home safer, helping to prevent accidents and create character.

The following conditions each require different lighting solutions.

Fixed-use space

Generally, kitchens, bathrooms and garages all have fixed lighting. you will want to balance fixed or ambient lighting with task lighting, providing light for chopping vegetables or washing dishes. On staircases, you should have lighting at the top to illuminate the stair treads. You should also have light at the front of the stair, to illuminate the stair riser and prevent shadows, which will help you read the depth and height of each step – helping you in not tripping up the stairs!

Multi-use space

Living rooms, open plan kitchen-dining rooms and bedrooms require more varied lighting for different uses and atmospheres. Successful lighting mixes in these rooms will be flexible, with, for example, spot lighting for reading, or wall lighting for the illumination of shelving displays. This 'task' lighting will need to be supplemented by ambient lighting, so as to reduce glare.

Outdoor space

While single, fixed lighting will suffice in service spaces such as driveways and porches, you will probably want more flexible lighting in your patio and/or garden. This will enable you to create character, or changing the lighting mood according to the setting or needs of a specific area. Lighting levels in these areas can be quite low, as a little light will go a lot further outdoors than in.

Fixed-use space

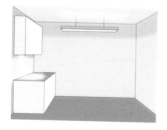

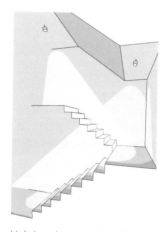

The light on the ceiling gives good ambient light, whilst a strip light or spot light mounted above a counter will give good localised light.

Lighting above a stair will light the treads and landing. Lighting from the front will help illuminate the risers, making them safer.

Outdoor space

Fixed light will be sufficient for walkways and porches though a spot light above a patio can provide more flexible and direct lighting.

Multi-use space

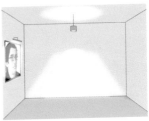

A pendant light provides good general lighting and reflected light off the ceiling. Wall mounted light fittings above pictures give very pronounced light where it is needed.

The recessed ceiling light gives restricted light with very pronounced downward shadowing. Additional task lighting may be needed in a multi-use space.

WHAT TO ASK

→ Where does the sun rise and set.

→ Does the property have any problems with either overheating in the summer or being overshadowed by neighbouring buildings.

WHAT TO LOOK FOR

→ Visit at different times of day to find out how changing light affects the property.

→ Are rooms generously glazed to allow good natural light.

→ Look to see if there might be any problems of overlooking from neighbouring properties.

→ Check there is potential for a good range of flexible artificial lighting to suit your needs.

FITTINGS

It is more important that you buy the best space you can get rather than worry too much about fixtures and fittings. Property purchase is about buying the best performance shell you can afford; the knobs and knockers you can always change later. Don't be fooled by a property that has a flashy oven or cupboard handles that cost more than you thought you could afford. It may be that the property builder has skimped on the specification of windows or doors or disguised cheap brickwork with concrete render and is hiding the fact by wowing you with nice ironmongery.

Having said that there is a standard in quality that you should expect and ask for. If not sensibly designed, permanent fittings can spoil the appearance and appeal of your home.

Just as you do when buying a new car, when buying a new home you should be able to negotiate the level, and quality, of the fittings before you buy. Whether it is kitchen facilities or sanitary fittings, prepare a list of all your requirements before viewing a property.

Low-E glass

Everyone knows that double-glazing can reduce heat loss. The use of low emissivity glass – often referred to as Low-E glass – will save you even more energy. And you will save even more energy still if argon is enclosed between the layers of glass instead of air.

WHAT TO ASK

→ What fittings and features are included in the price.

→ What choices are available for worktops, kitchen units, sanitary ware, tiling, etc..

→ What warranties are provided on ironmongery and fittings.

→ If there is an open fire, are there any limitations on the fuel that can be burnt.

Turn it off

Have you ever had one of those moments when you come downstairs in the morning and find the kitchen flooded in four inches of water? And when you desperately need to turn the mains supply off, but can't remember where the stop cock is? Before you buy your new home, make sure you ask the location of the mains water supply and the stop valve for the cold water storage tank. If there is a leak in the future, knowing where they are could save you money, time and embarrassment.

Tomorrow's world

Interactive fridges, robots that hoover your carpets, light-sensitive lighting systems – while some inventions never see the light of day, it is worth thinking about your immediate technological needs. Does your new home have broadband access? Will you be able to receive a digital TV signal when the analogue signal is turned off? Can you create home networks for your TV, computer and music system easily? One easy step to take here is to count the number and location of phone points – will they suffice for your needs?

WHAT TO LOOK FOR

→ Are drains and gutters clean and in working order.

→ Are all the appliances that are supplied with the house connected and ready to use.

→ Check to see if the house is fitted with mains operated smoke detectors with a back up battery.

→ Check that there are adequate power points and that they're in the right place.

→ If you have a shared entrance, check to see how people enter the building. Is there a door viewer to help you see who is at the door.

→ Can blinds and curtains be easily fixed over windows.

BUYING OFF-PLAN

Buying 'off-plan' is when you buy a property that hasn't been built yet but where the developer has plans and has started to build. You will be able to view a show home, look over plans and a model, or various artist's impressions of the development. However, you won't actually be able to see inside the home that you may want to buy.

It takes a certain leap of faith to buy off-plan without being able to see the finished product. Buying off-plan may allow you to get a home at a good price and in the position you want. And it should give you greater scope to influence the choice of fittings and finishes.

Architectural plans are a lot more complex than the one on the Cluedo board. Whilst Cluedo has a library, drawing room

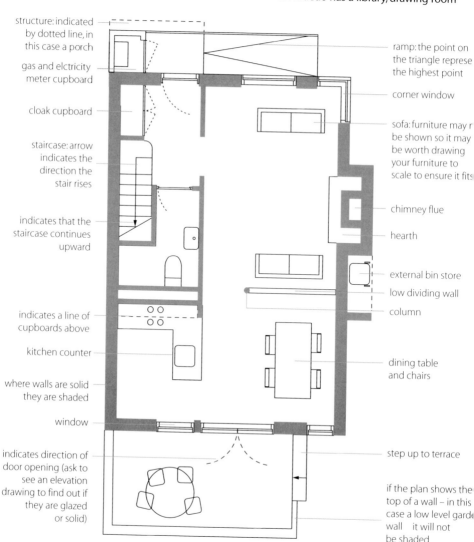

structure: indicated by dotted line, in this case a porch

gas and elctricity meter cupboard

cloak cupboard

staircase: arrow indicates the direction the stair rises

indicates that the staircase continues upward

indicates a line of cupboards above

kitchen counter

where walls are solid they are shaded

window

indicates direction of door opening (ask to see an elevation drawing to find out if they are glazed or solid)

ramp: the point on the triangle represe the highest point

corner window

sofa: furniture may r be shown so it may be worth drawing your furniture to scale to ensure it fits

chimney flue

hearth

external bin store

low dividing wall

column

dining table and chairs

step up to terrace

if the plan shows the top of a wall – in this case a low level garde wall it will not be shaded

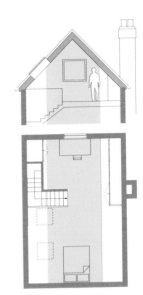

and parlour it doesn't show where the boiler will be, which way doors swing open and the size and shape of windows. Nor does it tell you whether you will be able to fit a bed, wardrobe and desk in the bedroom, and still be able to walk around them. Above all else, then, make sure you understand the plan.

Plans in marketing brochures tend to be indicative. Room sizes, window positions or even the position of walls may be different in the final built scheme. You should, therefore, insist on seeing the architect's construction plans or a detailed model, as these will more accurately represent what you are thinking of buying.

Similarly, here, it is just as important to see and understand a sectional drawing – remembering that the height of a room will affect its quality. If the roof space, for example, is used for a room the plan may look generous. A section, however, will give you a better sense of the actual space as it will show the slope of the roof and how that affects the usable floor area and where you are going to be able to stand up without banging your head.

area with adequate head clearance

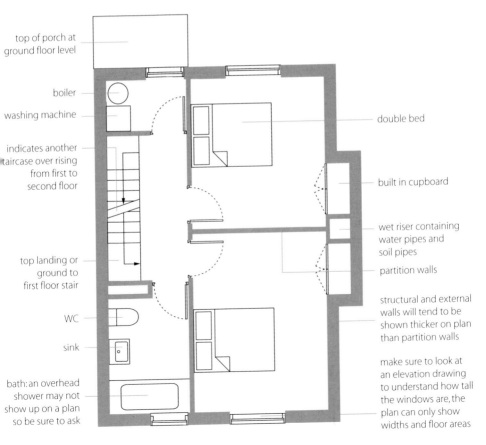

top of porch at ground floor level

boiler

washing machine

indicates another staircase over rising from first to second floor

top landing or ground to first floor stair

WC

sink

bath: an overhead shower may not show up on a plan so be sure to ask

double bed

built in cupboard

wet riser containing water pipes and soil pipes

partition walls

structural and external walls will tend to be shown thicker on plan than partition walls

make sure to look at an elevation drawing to understand how tall the windows are, the plan can only show widths and floor areas

Finally, you will need to find out whether there are any future developments that might affect your new home. The relevant local authority will have a record of any proposed development plans, as well as any planning applications that might affect your new home. If your property is part of a larger development find out what the phasing programme is and how long you will have to put up with living next to a building site.

Occupy, circulate, appropriate

When viewing a potential home, always remember to think about how you will occupy it, how you will move through it and how you might appropriate it to suit your own needs.

If you are happy with all of your enquiries, then you should be ready to put pen to paper and buy your off-plan home. Your developer will ask you to sign a reservation form, giving them a clear commitment from you to purchase the property. Make sure you get a commitment from them, including a completion date, and a break clause or amount of compensation if this date is not met. Don't assume that this is automatically offered. Many volume home builders do not guarantee a completion date when exchanging contracts and it will require tenacity and determination to negotiate a reduction in price at a later date if there are delays.

When you sign there will be typically four stages of payment. The first will be a reservation fee which should never be more than a fraction of 1 per cent of the value of the property. On exchange of contract you will usually pay around 5 per cent, and another 5 per cent when the walls and roof of the property have been completed. The balance will ordinarily be due on completion. The developer may try to tie you into the purchase by offering to return the deposit if the house is not completed over a year after the initial date indicated. There are often many legitimate reasons for delays to building works – for example, adverse weather conditions – but if you were privately commissioning a builder to build you a home within a certain period you would contractually agree penalties for late completion. There is no reason why developers can't offer a similar deal to their customers.

Once a completion date has been agreed, ask the builder to give you monthly construction progress reports. These should help you manage the project from your side.

When the home is completed make sure it has been built as set out in the plans and that a window isn't mysteriously missing where one was proposed or the finishes aren't quite what was promised. It does happen!

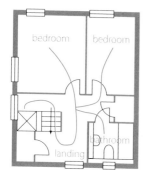

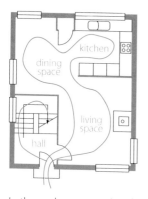

In these plans we see how open plan living has been introduced on the ground floor with more conventional arrangements above.

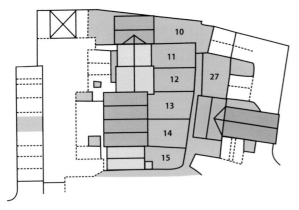

On the boundary

When you're examining the plans, make sure that you are clear about the location of the property boundaries. It is always a good idea to 'walk the plot', which is developer speak for walking around the development to get a clear idea of where your home will be situated and how it will be orientated. You should also use this visit to clarify the location of the property boundaries, so as to be sure to avoid costly disputes at a later date. You should ask your developer to keep you informed of any changes to the boundaries – however minor – that might occur during the build phase of the development.

Adoption

During the construction of a development, streets and footpaths are often under the control of the developer. Subsequently, they are usually 'adopted' by the local authority, who thereby takes responsibility for cleaning and maintaining them. If the streets and footpaths on your development are privately owned you should be wary, as you may be liable for a share of their maintenance costs. If so, find out what the level of maintenance cost will be before going any further with your potential purchase.

Jump the queue

Units in a large new housing development with several phases are often sold, in the first phase, up to 10 per cent cheaper than in the second so as to generate sales momentum. So, if you want a bargain get to the head of the queue.

WHAT TO ASK

→ Who are the architects. What other projects have the developer and architect built and can you visit them. Do you like them.

→ Can you have a copy of the specification for your property. This will help you keep a record of what the developer should provide.

→ Ask to see computer generated visuals of each room and the property in its entirety.

→ Where will the boiler and key plumbing or electrical installations be located. Will they be easily accessible for maintenance.

WHAT TO LOOK FOR

→ Look at samples of fittings and features that are going to be included in the property, and then either record these photographically or get the relevant catalogues.

→ Be wary of furniture in show homes. If furniture is of non-standard size (for example, if short beds are used), it will give a misleading impression of the size and space of the property.

→ Will there be adequate power points and are they in the right places.

→ Ensure there is space to accommodate furniture that may not be displayed in the show home. For example, wardrobes may be missing to give the impression of more space.

SALES AND AFTER SALES CARE

Did you know that there is a league table for home builders, ranked by level of customer satisfaction? Published by the *Housing Forum*, the performance table is based on a variety of issues, including quality, construction, value for money, service levels and after sales service.

WHAT TO ASK

→ Does the builder offer after sales service and customer care.

→ Is there a management company.

→ What are the management charges, service charges and ground rent and what do they cover.

→ How will communal areas, stairs, lifts and gardens be maintained.

→ What are the builder's procedures for defects.

→ What maintenance response facility does the builder provide.

A home builder's job doesn't just stop once the property has been constructed. For apartments or developments with shared amenities, you need to make sure that they have put in place an efficient management system to maintain the properties, enhance the landscaping and manage the shared amenities. Often this may require a full-time concierge or on-site caretaker. The builder may also help you set up a residents committee to liaise with the management company. In addition they have a responsibility for dealing with defects.

For some reason new homes are exempt from the Sale of Goods Act 1994, which means there are few consumer rights for the purchaser of a new home. In other words, you can't take it back or get a refund. It is important to know what you can and cannot expect from your builder after you have bought your home, especially as a 2003 MORI poll showed that 90 per cent of new homes have snags and defects.

Before you move in, you should inspect the newly-built property and check for any defects. If there are any, you will need to establish who is responsible. The builder is responsible for correcting defaults that are the result of poor workmanship and you should write to them as soon as they appear requesting repairs. Typical defects include faulty plumbing, such as leaking cisterns or WCs, poorly connected pipes to sinks or boilers, plaster settlement cracks or nail popping – that is where nails used to fix plasterboard to timber joists or studs get pushed out. They will not cover wear or tear or condensation. Nor does it cover damage caused by shrinkage or thermal movement between materials, though if this resulted in structural damage you should have a case.

New homes should have a NHBC 'Buildmark Cover' or similar warranty to cover against defects for a period of two years and structural defects for a period of ten years. This is not the same as a warranty on consumer products which protect you from product failure of virtually any kind. A warranty on a house is in fact a latent defects liability insurance policy with strict terms of cover, so check with the NHBC or other insurers, like Zurich, as to what the terms of cover are.

NHBC has an online checklist that you can use to assess workmanship. While it is a useful list, it doesn't cover a number of hidden issues, like foundations, adequate installation of damp proof courses or insulation. These should have been checked by the NHBC inspector and Local Authority Building Control inspector during construction. The insurance will also cover arbitration should there be any dispute over defects, although it is hard to see who other than the home builder would be responsible. Insurance policies may not cover problems resulting from any alteration or extension that you undertake such as removing a partition or adding a conservatory or porch. The reason is that works, if poorly done, may damage or adversely affect your home by causing damage to foundations, drainage or damp proofing.

The best home builders won't let you complete on the mortgage until your *snagging* list has been dealt with and signed off. If the completion of the contract is towards the end of the financial year, some builders might pressurise you to complete the contract, to suit their accounts. The rule of thumb is simple – don't complete on an incomplete property. The NHBC and Zurich do not issue confirmation to mortgage lenders to issue monies until the builder can prove the home buyer has signed-off completion of the home. You should shop around and locate reputable builders who will fix problems before you commit to 25 years of debt.

They should return to the property a year after it is completed to conduct a full inspection, and rectify any defects caused by either workmanship or manufacturing defects. There are independent organisations, such as Inspector Homes, that offer a service to inspect new properties for defects before completion and up to the end of the typical two year warranty. In addition, they will negotiate with the builder on your behalf to ensure you get a fair resolution.

If you are buying an apartment or maisonette be sure you are clear who is responsible for maintenance and repairs. If a crack appears in your top floor apartment, and the ground floor has to be underpinned to remedy the crack, do you know who foots the bill? If you share the freehold, then you are likely to have to share the costs of any external or structural works, for example repairing the roof or redecorating the outside of the property. If you are a leaseholder, ask the freeholder about their obligations, and their level of insurance cover.

OUTDOOR
SPACE

YOU HAVE CHOSEN A HOME IN THE RIGHT
LOCATION AND YOU ARE SET TO COMMIT
PEN TO PAPER. BEFORE YOU DO, YOU
SHOULD THINK ABOUT THE IMMEDIATE
SPACE OUTSIDE OF THE PROPERTY –
FROM WHERE TO KEEP YOUR BIN TO
PLACES FOR PLANTING AND PLAYING.

OUTDOOR SPACE

Many of us aspire to life in a rural idyll, surrounded by greenery and fresh air. However, most of us would also rather live in a community than in isolation. We want convenience, whether that is being able to walk to a local shop or not having to spend three hours commuting to work. And because most of us end up living in a built-up neighbourhood, the quality of our immediate outdoor space is crucial in making it an enjoyable experience.

A built-up neighbourhood needn't deprive you of access to good public space. In fact it is worth remembering that good public space will contribute to your investment. Well planned and well managed public space has a positive impact on the value of nearby domestic properties. Research in The Netherlands, for instance, points towards a 6 per cent increase in a home's price if there is a good park nearby, with an 8 per cent increase if you have a view of it. In Berlin proximity to playgrounds in residential areas was found to increase land values by up to 16 per cent.

And you should not, of course, forget the health benefits in all this. Access to good quality, well maintained public spaces can help improve our physical and mental health by encouraging us to walk more, play sports, or simply enjoy a green and natural environment.

The quality of a neighbourhood will be partly determined by the calibre of its public spaces, squares and parks. The quality of the open spaces immediately surrounding your home, including private and shared gardens, off-street parking facilities and driveways is just as important. A home should be more than just a building lost in a sea of asphalt or grass. A well-designed home will be intrinsically connected to the space around it.

Another way to get an idea of what does and doesn't work with outdoor space is to think of it as an outdoor room. Thus, the outdoor space should be framed, just as a room is, whether it is with hedges, fences or other buildings. Similarly, communal gardens work when they are planned with specific social and cultural activities in mind, such as play, pleasure or planting. Undifferentiated, empty spaces, on the other hand, are more likely to end up neglected and potentially vandalised.

Boundaries

Open spaces around tower blocks are often unused and unloved. Part of the reason for this is because of the lack of definition over their boundaries, which often means that they generate no sense of ownership. The lack of a defined boundary also makes it unclear as to which neighbourhood they belong. Successful communal spaces are those that are well defined and landscaped.

BEYOND THE FRONT DOOR

Gates

The way in which the space between your home and the street is designed will have an impact on your sense of privacy and security. A well-designed 'threshold' or buffer zone will create a clearly defined boundary between the public realm of the street and the private realm of your house. This can be achieved either through landscaping or, more typically, through fences and gates.

Putting up gates around a whole development is often presented as a solution to problems of crime. More often than not, however, it ends up exacerbating the problem, isolating communities and creating *social exclusion*. While making your home secure is clearly important, there are less aggressive means to making your neighbourhood safe than encircling it in razor wire and having CCTV cameras on every street corner. You are better off having an active relationship between home, street and community.

Historically, properties built close to the street had steps up to their front doors. This has the advantage of rooms being raised above the eye level of people walking past, thereby creating a sense of privacy for the home owner. At the same time, it provides the passer-by with a sense of security, knowing that someone is looking over the street, potentially keeping an eye out for any incidents.

In the twenty-first century, the use of steps has decreased and architects have had to find other ways of creating that sense of privacy for the home owner, one method of which is a carefully designed set-back from the street. However it is achieved, the aim is to create a well-balanced buffer zone, that gives you a sense of security, but doesn't alienate you from your immediate neighbours.

A well defined space in front of a house sets clear boundaries between what is public and what is private.

In these poorly designed developments, shown above, the ownership of the front garden is unclear and there is no sense of privacy for ground floor rooms.

By contrast, the properties shown in the photos below do have a well defined sense of where the public space ends and private space begins.

Garbage

The average household generates 1.2 tonnes of rubbish every year. Imagine if you only had it collected once a year – where would you store it all? Thankfully, your bins are usually emptied once a week. Where they are kept in the meantime is, however, an issue.

Homes have somewhere to put your furniture, somewhere to put your washing machine and your bathtub, but rarely somewhere to put your bin. More often than not, it ends up in your front garden, meaning that it is the last thing you see when you leave the house in the morning, and the first thing you see when you return at night.

Some of the best homes are now being designed with external bin storage in mind. A well-designed bin store will be easy for you to access, but difficult for rats or other vermin to get into. A bin store should be hygienic and visually unobtrusive.

Utility meters

These are rarely well integrated into a design. More often than not, they will be white or brown boxes stuck on the outside of a building. We would not tolerate a similar level of bad design in a car – where, for example, the fuel gauge is tastefully integrated into the dashboard – so why tolerate it on something that is going to cost you considerably more money? An intelligent design solution should integrate the meters into an easily accessible cupboard, which might also be large enough to store a garbage bin or bicycle.

→ Who is responsible for the upkeep of fences or hedges that sit on a boundary with a neighbour.

→ How efficient is the provision of rubbish collection.

→ Does the local authority provide a recycling service. Or is this provided by a local business.

→ How close are the nearest recycling facilities.

→ Check to see whether there is a clearly defined boundary between your private space and the public space.

→ Look out for good exterior lighting.

→ Unobtrusive space or storage for rubbish bins.

Thoughtless positioning of garbage bins means that residents have to pass through a corridor of rubbish and dumped appliances to reach their front door.

Here in the Chronos development, London, storage sheds for rubbish and utility meters are integrated into the overall design plan allowing easy street level access for refuse collection. Off street parking is also successfully integrated into the overall ground plan.

THE GREAT OUTDOORS

Play

It would be wrong to suggest that a communal garden or play area can be the basis for building a community; nonetheless shared communal space will still have a bearing on the quality of our living environment and can make a place delightful and enjoyable.

The five-a-side football pitch or children's playground offer local social and recreational space. Any space between buildings can be put to some use if considered from the outset. How often have you seen signs saying 'no ball games' or 'keep off the grass'? Such mean mindedness results in open spaces being merely for visual effect, wasted and often neglected. Admittedly, ball games won't be desirable in some spaces, so the question here should be, is there provision in the neighbourhood for games to take place?

Play is crucial for many aspects of children's development.

Beaufort Court, in London, has a basketball court in its central courtyard, which has swiftly become the focal point of activity – the urban equivalent of the village cricket green. More common to most developments is a communal playground where children can meet safely and securely, being overlooked by neighbouring homes.

When choosing your new home, be sure to list your children's preferences as well as your own. Access to good outdoor space can improve health and well-being and arguably help tackle the frightening statistic that 30 per cent of school children are overweight. Over 65 per cent of nine to 11 year olds are dissatisfied with the quality of outdoor play areas whilst 94 per cent of kids want to spend more time playing outside their homes. And good outdoor play space isn't just for the kids – nearly 90 per cent of parents would prefer to play outside with their children than watch TV.

WHAT TO ASK

→ How are play areas managed, are they secured at night and is there agreement about who can use them and when.

→ Who is responsible for their upkeep and maintenance.

→ Is this covered by your service charge.

WHAT TO LOOK FOR

→ Check to see whether there is a clear definition between communal public areas and any private gardens on their borders.

→ Will you be able to see or supervise your children in the communal playing area from the windows of your home.

Basketball at Beaufort Court.

Leisure

Every home should have access to some outdoor space, whether it is a private balcony, a private garden, or a shared garden. There are some great examples of housing developments offering both private garden space and shared open space for residents. A typical Georgian Square includes small private protected back gardens and a shared garden square at the front of the house. The square serves as a supplement to the private gardens, while also acting as a focus for community life. The village green works in a similar fashion, with houses surrounding a communal public space – though in this case, the green can be enjoyed by everyone, not just the residents. Community gardens bring people together from different ages and cultures helping to create a real sense of neighbourhood.

In the award-winning Iroko development in London, ground floor apartments have private gardens, which open onto a landscaped communal garden shared by all the residents. This model is often used in other European countries, and offers better security because the positioning of the communal garden at the backs of the houses provides better protection from the street. This sense of security is increased by it being overlooked by the apartments – although this might not offer as much peace and quiet as the 'village green' model. In order to overcome this problem, the residents of Iroko have agreed and signed up to a set of principles defining times of use, acceptable levels of noise and strategies for dealing with anti-social behaviour.

The green space around your home should be used wisely and effectively – and not just as an afterthought once car parking decisions have been made. Remember that the price you pay for your home also includes the land around it – so make sure you maximise it for your own pleasure and delight.

On the ground

Where gardens or landscapes are shared, ground floor apartments should have direct access to them. Too often, the plans for ground floor apartments are the same as for those on the upper levels, necessitating access to the garden through a shared staircase. With the creation of a proper threshold, there is no reason why ground floor apartments shouldn't feel safe opening onto a communal garden.

WHAT TO ASK

→ Are there any restrictions on the use of outdoor space, whether it is in having barbecues, ball games, or hanging out your washing to dry.

→ What management is in place to look after communal spaces.

WHAT TO LOOK FOR

→ The landscaping should be appealing and designed to be durable.

→ Will you be able to fit a table and chairs on the balcony – or just a couple of plant pots.

→ Check whether private balconies have dedicated drainage so that when you water your plants you don't soak you neighbour sitting out below.

WHAT TO ASK

→ What is the condition of the ground.

→ What type of soil is it.

→ Will this affect the type of plants that can grow.

→ If plants are already provided what sort of care is needed.

WHAT TO LOOK FOR

→ Dig around to check that the garden is not a thin layer of topsoil over builder's rubble, or clinker.

→ Check to see whether there is a rainwater butt, which is an environmentally efficient way of watering the garden or cleaning the car.

→ The garden should be sheltered from prevailing winds.

→ The planting should be appropriate for the amount of sun or shade in the garden.

→ There should be storage for your gardening equipment.

→ Check for puddles on the patio or paved areas as this may indicate poor run-off and drainage.

Gardens

Creating a garden from scratch – whether it is building a patio or erecting a trellis – can be an expensive business, so it is worth finding out what is included with your home. Although some developments – for example, Lacuna in Kent – include fully landscaped gardens, with patios and planting already in place, this isn't the norm.

If you enjoy gardening it is worth finding out what condition the ground was in before your home was built, and what has been done to improve it. Six out of ten new developments are on *brownfield* sites, which means land that either used to have domestic or industrial buildings on it, or was unused urban land. Some *brownfield* sites are on land which has been polluted with contaminants. There are, however, regulations in place to ensure these sites are cleaned before development begins.

Three factors will influence how well your plants will flourish: the soil; the amount of moisture available; and the amount of sun. A new garden should have at least six inches of good quality topsoil. And underneath this topsoil you will want more than just builder's rubble. The builder should be able to tell you about the quality of the subsoil, and whether they have provided adequate drainage or run-off.

When thinking about where to position your plants, remember that large plants near to the building will affect the quality of light entering your home. Similarly, trees can provide useful shade in the summer, and allow additional light into the property in the winter once their leaves have fallen.

As urban living becomes more popular some new developments are including well designed and highly planted gardens. If you have to compromise on the number of rooms you can afford, a small garden can become a valuable outdoor room. You will get the most out of your garden if it is sheltered, sunny and well planted.

CAR PARKING

Convenience or community

For the sake of convenience we would all like to be able to park outside our front door, whether to make it easier to carry in the shopping or get the children into the car, but once we have parked, we don't want the car to dominate the street scene or to detract from the character of the area.

Badly designed car parking will not only impact on the amount of land available, but can also affect our relationship with our neighbours. Badly designed homes – particularly if they have a lack of storage – will result in bicycles, lawn mowers, workbenches or the chest freezer being confined to the garage, and the car being evicted onto the street. This can put pressure on visitor parking spaces or result in disputes caused by blocked access points.

Many well-designed housing developments now offer off-road parking in shared parking areas or, in the case of urban developments, underground. As long as these are efficiently designed, they will free up space for a more attractive streetscape, more communal public areas and more efficient use of our limited land resource.

Too much of the time, we worry unnecessarily about the secure parking of our cars, insisting that we should be able to park it as close as possible to our home. Statistics, however, show that the design of more secure cars has resulted in a halving in the number of motor vehicles being stolen during the period between 1991 to 2003. The theft from vehicles in the same period has dropped by a third. Given that 'theft from the person of another' has increased almost fourfold and violent crime is up from 265,000 to 992,000 incidents, the security and design of our neighbourhoods would seem to be a more pressing problem than where you can park your car.

WHAT TO ASK

→ Are there any parking restrictions.

→ Who is responsible for policing the parking.

→ What visitor parking is provided.

→ If car parking is shared or underground how is this controlled and secured.

The design of car parking needs to be as well considered as any other part of a development. The schemes pictured here offer a variety of parking solutions other than the ubiquitous garage that dominates the front of many properties. They include parking courts, mews garages, well landscaped parking bays, sheltered car ports and underground car parking.

WHAT TO LOOK FOR

→ Car parking should be sensitively integrated and designed so as not to dominate the street.

→ There should be sufficient space and water in case you want to wash or repair the car in its parking area.

→ If there is plenty of parking when you visit during the day, return in the evening to see how it changes as people return from work.

→ Is the garage wide enough or long enough to comfortably get children, prams and shopping out.

→ Will you need to store things other than your car in your garage – workbench, bicycles, lawnmower, and will they fit.

WHERE TO GO FROM HERE

HAVING ABSORBED THE INFORMATION IN THIS GUIDE YOU ARE READY TO HUNT FOR A NEW HOME WITH CONFIDENCE. NOW IS THE TIME TO PREPARE YOURSELF WITH OUR READY-MADE LIST OF QUESTIONS AND START SEARCHING.

A BUILDING IS FOR LIFE

The purchase of your home is the largest single capital investment you'll make during your life, so you need to consider both the product and its context. There are, of course, a range of other considerations to be made when buying a home, for example, how to get a mortgage and appoint a solicitor, but these procedural matters are beyond the scope of this guide. The Council of Mortgage Lenders and The Law Society are best placed to give advice on these issues.

This guide has set out many of the things that you need to consider when looking to buy a well-designed home. Its advice is not a substitute, however, for having a professional survey carried out, which a mortgage lender will require. If you incorporate design into your considerations at the beginning of your home-buying process, then the chances are you won't need either a feng shui consultant or a TV personality to redress its faults once you've moved in. This might mean that you come across as demanding to prospective vendors, whether they are builders, architects or home owners. Better, though, to be informed now, than to be disappointed – and in debt – later.

You might decide that you can leave some of the issues discussed in this guide until a later date. Remember, though, that if you are planning to sell the property in the future, other people might be more demanding than you have been. So, a well-designed home will not only make your life more enjoyable in the short term, it will also make your life less stressful in the longer term.

Building for Life

Building for Life is an initiative from the Commission for Architecture and the Built Environment (CABE), the House Builders Federation and The Civic Trust in association with Design for Homes. Its aims are:

- to identify great new housing schemes, both at home and abroad, and explain to the house building industry why these designs work so well and how they can learn from them

- to understand better the aspirations of people buying homes so that the design of new housing is more attractive to them

- to identify the barriers to designing quality new homes and campaign to remove them.

www.thehomebuyersguide.org, the associated website, offers information and advice to home buyers that complements the contents of this guide, including links to a wide variety of property sales websites, competitions and regular news features.

Awards

Building for Life awards Gold and Silver Standards to well-designed housing developments. Schemes that fulfil 70 per cent of the award criteria receive a Silver award, while those fulfiling 80 per cent are awarded the Gold standard.
For further information on the criteria used and to see whether there are any award-winning schemes near you, visit www.buildingforlife.org

"I DO NOT WANT MY HOUSE TO BE WALLED IN ON ALL SIDES AND MY WINDOWS TO BE STUFFED. I WANT THE CULTURES OF ALL THE LANDS TO BE BLOWN ABOUT MY HOUSE AS FREELY AS POSSIBLE. BUT I REFUSE TO BE BLOWN OFF MY FEET BY ANY."

Home Information Packs

The government is committed to making the home buying and selling process more transparent, clearer, faster and consumer friendly. At present, critical information, such as surveys and local searches only becomes available after negotiations have been completed and terms agreed. To improve the home buying and selling process this information needs to be supplied up front and, where possible, in a user-friendly format, so that consumers are better prepared before they make their decisions on whether or not to buy.

From January 2007, home owners or their selling agents will be required to have a home information pack that they will have to make available to prospective buyers on request. The packs will include information on terms of sale, evidence of title, replies to standard searches, planning consents, agreements and directions, building control certificates, warranties and guaranties, as well as a home condition report that includes an *energy efficiency* assessment.

Having this information available right from the start of the process will enable buyers and sellers to negotiate from an informed position. It will also help consumers commit more quickly to the transaction by increasing certainty and thus avoiding unwelcome surprises which currently cause renegotiations and costly transaction failures after terms have been agreed.

HAPPY HOUSE HUNTING

Property	1	2	3	4	5	6
Location						
The area should feel like a place rather than just a group of properties. Does it have a strong sense of identity?						
Is there housing in the area for a cross-section of people with a variety of needs?						
Does the area have well-designed streets and public spaces?						
Neighbourhood						
Does the area feel safe and is it easy to navigate by street and on foot?						
Do streets and pathways connect with the surrounding area?						
Is it well lit at night?						
Is there easy access to public transport?						
Is the property near local amenities, such as a shop, chemist, or post office?						
Are there local community facilities that you would use, such as a nursery, community hall or school?						
Position						
Is the property orientated to make the most of the sun?						
Do homes take priority over street layout and car parking?						

To help you hunt for a home, the table below provides a summary of the points that make for a successful and sustainable home.

Use the tables as a checklist to help you quickly and readily assess the design merits of any property, and its location.

roperty	1	2	3	4	5	6
windows look out over destrian routes and public areas extra security?						
es the home have *Secured by sign* accreditation or does it ccessfully adopt similar principles pen at the front, enclosed at e back)?						
ome design						
you know how the property is nstructed? Will it be easy to aintain? Is it adequately undproofed?						
es the property have rooms that an be put to different uses and can be adapted/converted/ expanded?						
the property well insulated and es it have other energy efficient atures such as double-glazing?						
there plenty of built-in storage?						
Outdoor space						
Does the property have access to rivate open space – a garden, balcony?						
Does the property have sensitively ntegrated car parking?						
Would you be proud to call his home?						

THE VALUE OF YOUR HOME

Once your neighbourhood criteria have been met you can assess how different properties compare in terms of value for money. With reference to the energy cost table below, follow the formula on the right hand table to calculate the value per sqm. For an example refer to page 59.

The energy table below represents a fuller version of the diagram on page 52.

Property Type	SAP	Yearly space and water heating costs	Carbon index
1900 Property as constructed with gas central heating fitted 20 years ago	27	£830	1.5
1900 Property with insulation improvements and standard gas central heating	57	£440	4.2
1900 Property with insulation improvements and condensing gas central heating	70	£338	5.4
New-build pre April 2002, with standard gas central heating	76	£300	5.9
New-build pre April 2002, with condensing gas central heating	82	£265	6.5
New-build post April 2002, with standard gas central heating	90	£230	7.2
New-build post April 2002, with condensing gas central heating	96	£200	7.8

The costs included do not take into consideration your own personal energy usage – if you leave the TV on all night and do lots of ironing, for instance – but they are very useful in comparing energy costs of equivalent properties.

The figures are based on a detached house with an area of 120sqm and with the same area of openings. Insulation improvements in the calculations were: loft – 200mm quilt, walls – 50mm insulation, glazing – 100 per cent double glazed 6mm air gap, draught proofing – 100 per cent, cylinder insulation – 100mm jacket, heating and controls – modern, gas heating with programmer, roomstat and *thermostatic valves*.

Note: The 1900 property was assumed to have solid walls, and while these can be insulated the cost of doing so may be prohibitive. (Data provided by the House Builders Federation and Elmhurst Energy Systems.)

These figures are indicative and should only be used for comparison purposes.

Property	1	2	3	4	5	6
Price						
Energy cost (see opposite) multiply by 10 for a ten year period						
Maintenance costs Add 2 per cent of market value if a period property and multiply by 10 for a ten year period						
Cumulative cost = i + ii + iii						
Floor area (sqm)						
Value for money – divide cumulative cost (A) by Floor area (B)						

GLOSSARY
& INDEX

WHAT TO SAY, HOW TO SAY IT
AND WHERE ELSE TO LOOK.

GLOSSARY

You will come across a few new terms in this guide (in italic) that you might not understand. Don't be put off. Here is what they mean.

Acoustic tests
Ensure that the sound insulation in a new house is sufficient. New houses should be built not only to reduce external noise, but also to prevent your neighbour from disturbing you, and you from disturbing your neighbour.

Aspect
Refers to the placing of the windows in a house. A double aspect house has windows that look out in more than one direction: a single aspect house has windows on only one side.

Brownfield sites
Are areas of land that have previously been developed, as opposed to 'greenfield' (land that has not been developed). A brownfield site may be green to look at if its buildings were demolished some time ago and the land has become overgrown.

Building regulations
Apply to most new buildings in England and Wales, and to extensions, alterations and change of use of existing buildings. They are designed to ensure that buildings are secure, structurally sound, safe in the event of fire, and a range of other criteria. Rather like a car's MOT, they are a minimum standard rather than a certificate of excellence.

Build specification
A document that sets out the requirements for how a new house will actually be built. It covers areas such as type and quality of materials, number of rooms, division of space within the house, as well as issues such as energy efficiency.

Carbon Index
A scale of measurement based on the annual level of carbon emissions (responsible for environmental damage) caused by heating your home and hot water. The index runs from 1 (bad) to 10 (good).

Condensing gas boiler
The most efficient and least polluting way of generating heat with gas.

Covenants
Conditions that can be attached to land or property when they are sold. They apply to all future owners of a property, and are used to prevent specific development or changes. For example, a covenant could prevent you from building an extension on your back garden.

Defects liability period
The length of time for which a house builder is responsible for correcting problems with a new house. This is usually two years for general defects, and ten years for structural defects.

Density per hectare
Refers to the number of homes per hectare. The average private new housing density is around 25 dwellings per hectare (12 per acre), a figure that has barely changed over the last two decades. The government has directed local authorities to avoid densities of less than 30 units per hectare and encourages densities in the 30-50 per hectare range.

Elevation
Is the architectural term for one side of a building or a room.

Energy efficiency
Is the aim of reducing the amount of fuel required to heat, cool, light and run a building. An energy rating (or NHER rating) is used to calculate the energy efficiency of a building, by measuring the costs of space and water heating as well as cooking, lights and appliances. On a scale from 0 to 10, an average dwelling would currently score between 4.5 and 5.5, with newly built homes nearer to 8 or more.

Ergonomic
Describes something that has been designed for ease of use.

Gob-on
A disrespectful term for non-functional decorative features that have been added to buildings purely for effect.

Hectare
Is the metric unit for measuring area. They have replaced acres (the imperial unit). A hectare is equivalent to 2.47 acres.

Insulation rating
A way of measuring the rate of heat loss through windows and insulation (also known as the U-value).

Intermediate ownership
Is offered by housing associations as a halfway option between renting and buying. It uses a combination of a mortgage with rent, or a separate loan.

Live/work units
Accommodation that is specifically designed to allow both residential and business use.

Mixed tenure
Where an area includes a combination of both types. Mixed tenure is believed to lead to more successful, less divided, communities.

Mixed use
Areas and buildings that contain a variety of different types of use. A mixed use building may have shops and restaurants on the ground floor and flats above.

Negative equity
Where the amount owed on a mortgage exceeds the value of the property.

Permeable
When applied to public space, this means an area that is easy to move through, because it has clear routes and signs, designed for simple navigation.

Pocket parks
Are usually developed from unwanted pieces of land, and created and run by local communities rather than the council. They are not necessarily small – their size depends on the piece of land involved.

Radburn principles
Radburn-type housing layouts take their name from a development at Burnham Place, Radburn, New Jersey, 1922-1933. Classic Radburn layouts are characterised by front and rear access, accommodating transport and pedestrian needs separately. Typically these would feature a road/garage side for vehicles and a footpath/'green' side for pedestrians.

SAP (Standard Assessment Procedure) rating
Based on annual energy costs for heating your home and hot water, producing a figure between 1 (bad) and 120 (good).

Secured by Design
A national police initiative supporting the principle that crime can be discouraged through design. Includes guidelines on various design issues, including access routes, landscaping, street lighting, and car parking.

Snagging
The inspection of building defects prior to sign off of final completion.

Social exclusion
The way that disadvantages, such as unemployment, poverty, lack of skills, can combine to push people out of mainstream society.

Sun space
An attachment to a building, such as a conservatory, that is designed to collect heat in sunny weather.

Sustainability
"Development that meets the needs of the present without compromising the ability of future generations to meet their own needs" (from 'Our Common Future', 1987). The key objectives of sustainability are:
- social progress that meets the needs of everyone
- effective protection of the environment
- prudent use of natural resources
- maintenance of high and stable levels of economic growth and employment.

Tenure
The way a building is owned or rented. There are three main variations:
- owner-occupied housing, where people own the houses in which they live
- social housing, which is rented housing supplied by a local council, or a housing association.
- intermediate ownership, see definition above.

Thermostatic valves
(thermostats) Allow the temperature of a heating system to be controlled.

Trickle vents
Small adjustable openings fitted to windows. If left in the open position, they help to control condensation while preventing heat escaping.

uPVC
Is short for Unplasticised polyvinyl chloride, a modern synthetic material used in the manufacture of window frames and doors. Its manufacture has a detrimental impact on the environment.

U values
The rate of heat loss is expressed in 'U values'. The lower the U value, the greater the thermal insulation and energy savings.

- The U value of single clear glass is 5.4
- With ordinary double glazing this improves to 2.8
- With Low-E glass it is reduced by over 1/3 to 1.9
- If argon gas is used to fill the air gap, the value is 1.6

VOCs (volatile organic compounds)
Carbon-based chemicals that evaporate easily at room temperature. As well as damaging the ozone layer, they have been linked to various types of cancer. The solvents found in paint are an example, and all paint must now be labelled with the level of VOCs it contains.

INDEX

ACKNOWLEDGEMENTS

Wayne Hemingway

Wayne is the Chairman of Building for Life, a joint initiative between CABE, the House Builders Federation and the Civic Trust. He is also a world-renowned designer, the founder of Red or Dead and has recently been working with George Wimpey on a number of housing projects.

Alex Ely MA RCA RIBA

Alex is an architect and partner at the award-winning architecture practice mae llp. He is also the Head of Sustainable Communities at the Commission for Architecture and the Built Environment (CABE). Alex advises government on housing policy and house builders and housing associations on design standards and best practice. He is a member of the Housing Forum's off-site manufacturers working group, a panel that advises government on the use of modern building methods in housing.

The author would like to thank Cheryl Markosky, Peter Swain, Richard Spencer and Tom Bolton for their contributions. And to Sian Every, Katherine Heaton and Miranda Westwood for their considerable help in the sourcing of photos.

The publisher would like to thank Elizabeth Redding for her editorial comments in the preparation of this book.

QUOTATIONS

Page 2, Eliel Saarinen

Page 11, Henry David Thoreau

Page 97, Mahatma Gandhi

Page 111, Ralph Waldo Emerson

PHOTOGRAPH AND ILLUSTRATION CREDITS

Images appear by kind permission of the following copyright holders.

Photographs

AMA Alexi Marmot Associates: Fulham Island 81

Emma Appleton/CABE: 43

Annabel Biles/CABE: 40, 81

Bill Dunster Architects: BedZed 53

Hélène Binet/Sergison Bates/Silvia Ullmayer: 38, 62, 63

Berkeley Homes: Brewery Square front cover, 43

Bramhall Blenkharn: Sylvan Development 43

Brand X Pictures/Alamy: 64

Bryant Homes: Grange View 5

Tim Brotherton/Featherstone Associates: 38

Dominic Burke/Alamy: 40

CABE/EDAW: 83

Martin Charles/Cartwright Pickard Architects: 4, 45

Lizzie Coombes/Heads Together Productions: The Methleys 25

Constock Images/Alamy: 64, 65, 72

Countryside Maritime: Fishing Village front cover, 15, 83

Countryside Properties: Abode 4, 15, 17, 54, 66, 93; South at Didsbury Point 60, 61, 91

Crest Nicholson: Ingress Park 11, 15, 30, 37, 94

James Davies English Heritage NMR: Abbotts Cottages 10, 42; Century Court 11

Design for Homes: 62, Fulham Island: 30

Wayne Duerden/Department for Transport: The Methleys: 26

Mark Ellis & Ashley Bingham @ ICD Ltd: Front cover, 25, 71, 81, 86, 87; Bishops Mead 15, 37, 93; Chronos 85, 93; Millers Yard 102; Rivermead 8; The Point 80; Thorley Lane front cover, 43

Alex Ely/CABE: 7, 18, 20, 21, 22, 27, 35, 40, 43, 56, 81, 83, 85, 86

Sabine Engelhardt: Homes and work for change: 40, 41

Environ Sunley: Lacuna: 31, 34, 35, 45, 91

Richard Fitch/Energy Saving Trust: Thermal images, 50

The garden picture library/Alamy: 78, 90

Katy Ghahremani and Michael Kohn: Hanger House 48

Goddard Manton: 91

Amos Goldreich/Feilden Clegg Bradley: Beaufort Court 87

David Grandorge/Zombory-Moldovan Moore: New House, County Cork 7, 32, 61

Paul Grundy: St James's Park 24

Linda Hancock: BedZed 29

Katherine Heaton/CABE: 82, 88

Wayne Hemingway: front cover, 25, 83, 84, 88

Hopkins Homes: Bishops Walk 43, 74

Michael Howe/mae llp: 60, 62

Keith Hunter Photography: Coulnakyle, Nethybridge 6, 39

Lucia Hutton/CABE: 41

ING Real Estate: Campbell Heights 55

Ingram Publishing/Alamy: 64,

Bridget Jones: Courtyard house 39

Peter Jenkins/CABE: front cover, 6, 17, 28, 66

Justin Kase/Alamy: 36

Linden Homes: Queen Elizabeth Park 22

Llewellyn Davies: 22, 23, 26, 30, 40, 82, 83, 92

London Aerial Photo Library: 14

mae llp: Lift up house 48

Manhattan Loft Corporation/Grant Smith: Fulham Island 18

Barry Mason/Alamy: 39

Joe Miles: 93

Maria Moore/The Chase: 14

Peter Neal/CABE: 21, 81, 89

Doug Norman/Alamy: 44

Paul Nunneley/Hoop Associates: 70, 82, 92

Sean O'Halloran/Hoop Associates: 34, 35, 49, 54, 61, 63, 70, 71

Justine Owen: Greenwich Millennium Village 82

Peabody Trust/Cartwright Pickard Architects/Yorkon: 45

PCKO Architects: Fishing Village 42

Plain picture/Alamy: 60

Roger Evans Associates: 17

Shepheard Epstein and Hunter: 66

Peter Stewart/CABE: 37

Adrian Taylor/FAT: Private House, Hackney 37

Adrian Trim: Morice Town 24

Nick Turner/Countryside Agency: 86

Paul Tyagi/Studio mg Architects: 28, 49

Urban Splash: Seedley and Langworthy 47

Urban Splash/Richard Cooper, Photoflex: The Collegiate front cover, 5, 10, 54; Timber Wharf 40, 54

Urban Splash/Trevor Burns Photography: Royal William Yard 62

Philip Vile/Haworth Tompkins: Coin Street: 81, 84, 89, 92

Morley von Sternberg/Haworth Tompkins: Coin Street 16

Miranda Westwood/CABE: 38

Nick White: Hockerton 28

K Whitcombe/Skyscan: 14

Illustrations

©Roger Evans Associates: 17

© Hoop Associates: 19, 30, 52, 74

© Alex Ely/mae llp: 20, 29, 31, 49, 51, 55, 57, 64-65, 67, 68-69, 72-73

CONTACTS

www.thehomebuyersguide.org

CABE
www.cabe.org.uk
t: 020 7960 2400
A public body that champions the creation of great buildings and public spaces. Through public campaigns and support to professionals, CABE encourages the development of well-designed homes, streets, parks, offices, schools, hospitals and other public buildings in England.
For Wales: www.dcfw.org
For Scotland: www.futurescotland.org

The Civic Trust
www.civictrust.org.uk
t: 020 7170 4299
The Trust promotes progressive improvements in the quality of urban life for communities throughout the United Kingdom.

Council of Mortgage Lenders
www.cml.org.uk
t: 020 7437 0075
The trade association for mortgage lenders in the UK. It provides advice on taking out a mortgage.

Design for Homes
www.designforhomes.org
t: 08704 163 378
A not-for-profit company, set up to promote the value of good housing design within the industry. It has an online directory of architects involved in housing.

Energy Saving Trust
www.est.org.uk
t: 020 7222 0101
An organisation established by the Government to promote energy efficiency to, businesses, local government and in the home.

House Builders Federation
www.hbf.co.uk
www.new-homes.co.uk
t: 020 7608 5100
This is the principal trade federation for private sector house builders in England and Wales.

The Housing Forum
www.constructingexcellence.org.uk/sectors/housing forum
t: 0845 605 5556
An organisation that promotes best practice in all aspects of housing construction and customer service.

Inspector Homes
www.inspectorhome.co.uk
t: 0845 051 1015
Inspector Homes specialise in checking new homes for defects throughout the UK, on behalf of home owners and property investors both before completion and up to the end of your 2 year warranty.

Institute of Plumbing
www.plumbers.org.uk
t: 01708 472 791
The UK's professional body for plumbers and the plumbing industry, providing advice on how to find a plumber you can rely on.

Land Registry
www.landreg.gov.uk
t: 020 7917 8888
The Government body that registers land in England and Wales, and records deals such as sales and mortgages.

The Law Society
www.lawsoc.org.uk
t: 0207 242 1222
The Law Society regulates and licenses all solicitors in England and Wales. It offers information and advice on choosing a solicitor.

The Leashold Advisory Service
www.lease-advice.org
t: 0845 345 1993
Provides free advice on the law affecting residential long leasehold property and commonhold.

National Association of Estate Agents
www.naea.co.uk
t: 01926 496 800
A professional organisation for estate agents, representing 10,000 members across the UK. It provides an online search facility to help you find an estate agent.

National House Building Council
www.nhbc.co.uk
t: 01494 735 363
An organisation that sets standards for new homes in the UK. It also provides insurance on new homes, and offer information on buying or building a new house.

Neighbourhood Statistics
www.neighbourhood.statistics.gov.uk
t: 0845 601 3034
This website provides easy access to statistics, including crime, health, and employment, for any neighbourhood in the UK.

Office of the Deputy Prime Minister (ODPM)
www.opdm.gov.uk/housing
t: 020 7944 4400
The Government department responsible for housing and planning. The housing section of their website includes fact sheets, statistics and guidance for home owners.

Office of the Ombudsman for Estate Agents
www.oea.co.uk
t: 01722 333 306
The ombudsman for people using estate agents. Around 800 firms participate in the scheme.

Royal Institute of British Architects (RIBA)
www.riba.org
t: 020 7580 5533
The membership body for architects in England and Wales. Its website provides listings to help you find an architect, and information about architecture.
For Scotland: www.rias.org

Royal Institution of Chartered Surveyors (RICS)
www.rics.org
t: 0870 333 1600
The membership and standard-setting organisation for chartered surveyors. It can help you find a qualified surveyor. Also covers Wales and Scotland.

Up My Street
www.upmystreet.com
A website providing information on your local area, similar to Neighbourhood Statistics (above). You can enter any postcode for information on issues such as crime, schools, and council performance.

World Wildlife Fund (WWF)
One Million Sustainable Homes Campaign
www.wwf.org.uk/sustainablehomes
t: 01483 426444
A global charity working to prevent degradation of the world's natural environment. Its One Million Sustainable Homes Campaign aims to reduce the environmental impact of new housing construction.

"A MAN BUILDS A FINE HOUSE; AND NOW HE HAS A MASTER, AND A TASK FOR LIFE; HE IS TO FURNISH, WATCH, SHOW IT, AND KEEP IT IN REPAIR, THE REST OF HIS DAYS."

Architecture Art Design
Fashion History Photography
Theory and Things